CW00448835

Stannard has suffered for being in the van of something. His poetry is innovative... in that it is primarily a poetry of ideas rather than of words and the textures of language. His insights continually perplex, he throws you off balance with disorientating perceptions, but there is always a strong thread of logic running through: his particular type of poetic logic. He doesn't see it as his first priority to put felicitous phrasings your way, though now and then he does, with humorous intent, or otherwise to prove a point. He has full use of the tools of the trade, but at the dinner table uses a knife and fork. He balances a street-slangy way of handling words with a precise and mock-classical mode that evokes laughter.

Often what he has to say is in the way of a puzzle, often it borders on the profound – but it always challenges you as to exactly how profound. It's baffling, in a good way. But never stale, that's one thing. This is poetry with the head fully engaged.

*Tears In The Fence*


One of the first paradoxes about Stannard is his ability to create complex conundrums with the most colloquial of vocabularies. His language is plain but his meaning isn't; he is intelligently silly and there are dark undercurrents to his tomfoolery. He celebrates the spontaneous in a style that is in fact highly crafted and artful.

Stannard works with word associations, which become word play; and with comic juxtapositions which are bathetic, surreal or surrealistically bathetic. At times his work has the eerie, mysterious quality of poetry in translation...

Perhaps the most succinct way to describe Stannard's work is as serious play. Each poem creates its own strange, but alluring fictional world.

*Scratch*

*The author writes:*

You know I hate to write about myself.

I think my poems are sometimes acts of explicit design and at other times products of chance and a subconscious activity I rarely understand. More usually they come from somewhere between these polarities. When asked to explain my poems I usually resort to taking on a puzzled or pained expression and say I can't speak at the moment because I have a terrible headache. When I *have* to explain my poems because there is a gun at my head I admit they sum up my life, in part or in whole, which is either exactly as it should be or very sad. I don't think of themes, I think themes are for others to find, but if the poems are my life then that's the theme, I suppose. Or one of them.

As for the biography you have a desire for, I seem to have been on this planet for a little over 48 years, and have been employed in a number of different occupations, including removing the internal organs from battery hens and a few hours as apprentice to a glamour photographer. I have shopped extensively in charity shops throughout the country, and am very much in love with a woman whose name is Ruth. My favourite TV programme is anything that features S Club 7 and the most recent record I bought was by The Dirty Three though by the time you read this it might have changed if The Flaming Lips bring out a new LP, which they probably won't, because they take 3 years to do a record. I've been writing poems for quite a long time but still have trouble with rhyme. My favourite food is with red wine; my big ambition is to be happy with my hair.

# Writing Down The Days

*– Stride –*

WRITING DOWN THE DAYS
© 2001 Martin Stannard
ISBN 1 900152 73 8

Cover design by Neil Annat

*Published by*
Stride Publications
11 Sylvan Road, Exeter
Devon EX4 6EW
England

www.stridebooks.co.uk

Stride Publications
85 Old Nashua Road
Londonderry, NH 03053
USA

www.stridebooks.com

southwest arts

# Writing Down The Days

*New and Selected Poems*

## Martin Stannard

# ACKNOWLEDGMENTS

Thanks are due to the editors who have published these poems before, in books and in magazines. In particular, I would like to thank Jim Vollmar of The Greylag Press for *Baffled In Nacton*; Ian Seed of The Bad Seed Press for *Something Cold and White*; Geoff Hattersley, a particular supporter through his magazine *The Wide Skirt*, and who published *The Flat of the Land* and *Denying England*; John Harvey, another who gave encouragement by publishing my work in *Slow Dancer*, and who published *The Gracing of Days*; Peter Sansom and Janet Fisher at Smith/Doorstop, who published *A Hundred of Happiness and Other Poems*, and who continue to give brilliant support; Phil Kirby, of The Waldean Press, for *Easter*; and printmaker Dale Devereaux Barker, with whom the poem 'From A Recluse To A'Roving I Will Go' was first published as a handmade limited edition artist/poet collaboration from his studio, otherwise known as The Shed.

'Arising' was written during December 2000 and January 2001, especially for this book.

Acknowledgement is also due two poets without whom I'm not sure what might have happened: Keith Dersley and Rupert Mallin. Thank you for long-lasting friendship whilst writing down the days.

And an especial thank you to Paul Violi, who has been a friend, a guide, an inspiration, and a supremely helpful critic – but above all else, a friend.

There are others I could and do thank for their support and encouragement along the way, and they know who they are and I'd hate to miss anyone out, which is why there is no list of names here – but they know who they are. Thank you.

And last, but by no means least, thanks to Rupert Loydell at Stride, for wanting to do this book.

Martin Stannard
July 2001

## Contents

ARISING
(New Poems, 2001)

## *Two Beds are Better than One*

When I was born I imagined that one day
I would get to be a railway worker
And that my son would turn out to be
A polemicist of the first order.

There were going to be oranges in the grove
And dole cheques for the employed
And the unemployed alike.
Everyone would know the difference
Between Frankie Laine and Frankie Vaughan
And Frankie Valli.

But I was not the father of my son,
And two beds are better than one at a push.
Some say that when a man tries to sell you
A sandwich he is acting out of the kindness
Of his heart. That is how we are today,
Believe me, that is how we are.

## The Night of Hooks

There was this stupendous dream
Of you opening letters and finding
FROGS.
The first deluge of the year was falling
As you unloaded the boat of children
And the bus conductor consulted the oracle
And said
NORTH, I RECKON.
You woke me to say the chair was falling apart
But all I could see was a ring of faces
So blank they might have been coins,
So crazy they might have been playing harmonicas.
Across the river
A light flickered in the window of the shack
Where we knew Greeks lived in poverty.
Tonight
You will hang up your breasts
And say it is
FOR GOOD. Why not FOR EVER?
The sound of ships far away suggested direction,
Not distance, I think.

## Workmen Working

Workmen are hammering dust
Insects are moving house so they can just fix up
     new shelves in them
*Who needs shelves across the sky?* I ask myself
But then that's why I am not a journeyman

You say *Workmen saw, artists bleat*
But then when I kept my mouth shut for two days
     you accused me of being numb
     in the heart and steel-veined
Yes, my face is an umbrella, but it is also
     a cathedral, a book and a psalm

Workmen are sawing logs
Girls the colour of escalators are forcing poems out
     of their wardrobes like earrings
*Who needs earrings when one can actually have the girl?*
     I ask myself
Yes, my ideas are alarms against the swim of things
But then that's why I grow fearful when waiting the results
     of medical checks: they have it in for us
     even after we have it out

## An Empty Summer

The weather was fragile. Pleasure boats sank
regularly out on the normally placid river.

The night before I had openly danced with a woman
plainly up for grabs. She was an American, I think.

The door had been propped open with a chair. A single
lamp lit the deserted room. Oh, Suffolk silences!

The surrounding fields lay draped under the ghostly air
that lured, then calmed, then committed treason.

The night before I had wanted a woman who had been
up for grabs but I was out of luck. I craved sympathy.

The furnishings and the unopened letters proffered
none. Everyone knew someone who was looking for work.

## Five Plums

### 1. Professor Plum and The Cold Snap

Dear old Professor Plum –
he saw this cold snap coming
long before we went out on the streets
and encountered ice.
'The world is not quite as we think,'
you said. But you understate it.

### 2. Professor Plum and The Professors

Professor Plum – how astute you are!
I agree: nowadays one has to watch what
one is saying if one is to avoid
blighting one's chances in the great
world of men, women, and professors.
But what can one do, Professor,
when one has all these pieces of paper?

### 3. Professor Plum and The Elixir of Youth

Oh Dr. Plum! What a changeable world
this is! It's so difficult to keep track
of things (to stay in touch with how
temperatures are rising on 'the streets')
and yet remain beautifully young.

### 4. Professor Plum and The Credibility Gap

Professor, the world is there, and I am over
here, and there is a gap. And in this gap
there is, well, I think some of them are sheep,
and I'm sure I spot some vegetables also,
plus some stuff I can't make out.
And I can't reach any of it. None of it.

*5. Professor Plum and The Bed*

He has seen my bed,
analysed my bed,
and imitated my bed.
So how come he is still unable to explain
any dream of mine in which
I seem to be enjoying myself?

## Concerning 'The Flat of the Land'

I had this poem
that started out being about
the blue sky.

Then a lot of people popped up in this poem.

So I had this poem about a lot of people
under a blue sky.

Then all my friends wanted to be in it.

I said, 'But there are a lot of people
in this poem already!'

'But we're your friends,' they said.

So I had this poem about a lot of people
including all my friends
under a blue sky.

Then I put some weather in it
because it was a British poem.

Then I put place in it
because people need place.

So I had this poem about a lot of people
including all my friends
under a blue sky
in some weather
at a particular place.

The poem was no longer about the blue sky,
and I called it 'The Flat of the Land'.

'But nothing happens in this poem,'
I heard someone say. 'It's so dull.'

So,
I had this dull poem.

## In God's Factory

I imagine myself stood in the queue for brains
In God's factory, and getting a raw deal it seems
To me. Mine never seems to function at full throttle
And recently the line between brain and tongue has
Got really fouled up, judging by what comes out
Of my mouth. Anyway, standing there in the queue
I see all sorts of famous people go by carrying
Their life-packs. The man who will invent the mirror
Walks through the hall, combing his hair into a mess.
The inventor of the canoe goes by, and I notice how
Short his legs are. A bunch of people are in a huddle
Over by the hot drinks dispenser, and someone tells
Me they are musicians plotting to take control of
The world's greatest auditoriums. The inventor
Of the pencil sharpener is a few places up from me,
Looking like he is going to be born needing a shave.
Eventually they hand me my brain, and tell me
To be sure to put it in the right way round.
Nobody bothers to say which way round that is.
While I am fumbling with my burden (a sign of things
To come, as it turns out) I see the man who will
One day design aviator shades having the same trouble.
None of the screws seem to fit the ready-drilled holes.
Someone saunters past looking really sophisticated:
I wonder who he is, and what he's going to do.
Suddenly it occurs to me there are no women around:
The room is full of men, and has a distinctive
Smell. A sign of things to come, as it turns out.

## The Ingredient

Teacups have it.
I don't know why teacups have it,
but teacups do.
Horses turned out into a cold field have it,
as do the smouldering remains of a bonfire.
Mugs do not have it. That's a certainty.
Sacks of coal at the back gate have it,
and jig-saw puzzles have it,
and a river meandering through life has it.
A canal seems to have it, but it hasn't.
A bike has it, if it is a very old bike.
Coloured pencils have it.
Leg irons are said to have it, but that's a joke,
and a very cruel joke at that.
This hasn't got it, but neither has a bottle of turps.
A Del Shannon 45 on the London label has it,
but a compilation LP of his Greatest Hits
doesn't have it although it's tried really hard.
Ham salad has it.
Or rather, ham salad can have it but it doesn't always.
Leather gauntlets have it, if they are brown leather gauntlets.
Discarded silk at the foot of the bed doesn't have it,
though sometimes it is worth pretending that it does.
Night has it, if it has been snowing.
The sea has it, even though it is saddened by oil,
and I am happy to live by the sea.
Aircraft do not have it.
Parks used to have it, but most have lost it
and are unlikely to regain that which has been squandered.
But ducks and swans have it. Especially swans.
And certain dreams have it.
Not all dreams, but certain dreams.
Some photographs have it.
Some photographs do not.
You do not have it, but not having it is not everything.
I rarely have it, and even when I do

it seems I am not quite myself.
Perhaps this explains how come teacups have it
and mugs do not.

## The World of Facts

The enemy is closing in.
I mean, the evening is closing
in. I can't make out your face
or the colour of the dress
you are probably wearing.
But I can
hear the traffic wearing out the street
so I must be near a terminus of humanity;
I can hear the clicking of heels
so I must be near a government office;
I can hear a cup of lukewarm tea going cold
so I must be near where the enemy closes in.

The cigarette has gone out.
I mean, the candle has gone
out. I can't make out your shape
or the cover of the magazine
you are always reading.
But I can
hear the steady drone of bees
so I must be near the wild and woody grove;
I can hear the hammering of a shark's head
so I must be within shouting distance
of the cliffed and craggy shore;
I can hear the denouement of a novel
so I must be near my wits' end.

The facts are closing in.
I mean, the facts are closing
in. I can see the trousers
you are wearing, and the sad mask
from your wardrobe of sad masks.
I can see the determination
of faces, so I must be out in the open.
I can see a grim sadness,
but this is simply

because I am in the world of grim facts.
I can see, however, that not all facts
are determinedly 'grim':
a fact among facts
is that there is a grim determination that,
mingled with almost indefensible high spirits,
doesn't give a damn whether the facts
are closing in or not.

## The Bed We Die On

A blanket of snow covers Suffolk,
Crisp and white. Today, Mr and Mrs Stannard

Are to be visited by H.R.H. Queen Elizabeth II
And they are busy putting out the flags

In anticipation. The children are sprucing
Themselves, for this is a great family occasion.

> *Dear Aubrey, the dresser you left us*
> *When you died looks tremendous in Jane's room.*
>
> *Is it an antique, or just really old?*
> *I really believe in protecting our heritage.*
>
> *But how damned English cold it is: thank God*
> *For those men who dig coal out of the ground.*
>
> *The Queen will understand why it is we greet her*
> *Wrapped in tufty scarves and wearing mittens.*

H.R.H. Queen Elizabeth II looks resplendent
And the Stannard family look okay also, and proud

As Suffolk Punches when Her Majesty runs a gloved
Finger along the rim of the dresser in Jane's room

And remarks upon the great qualities of British dust.
Then the monarch's eye is caught by the bed:

'What a beautiful old bed,' she says. And Mr Stannard
Replies, 'It's the bed the Stannards die on. Always

Have and always will, I hope.' The Queen is impressed,
And says something appropriate about Tradition.

## An Excursion In

Tomorrow is Wednesday, and a few light showers are forecast
In East Anglia so the Stannard family are planning not to have

A day out by the seaside, or to pay a visit to a nearby zoo
Where a selection of exotic animals are kept in tasteful

Confinement. Instead, and not unconnected with the fact that
Mr Stannard is just now going through one of those periods

When you try and stand back and appraise your position in
The world's melee, they will spend a fairly quiet day tidying

The junk in their shed. Perhaps they will treat themselves
To a Wimpy dinner to make a day in feel like a day out.

> *Dear Mum, I wish you were here. The low clouds*
> *Are filled with mystery: you can't see through them*
> *To beyond the end of your armful of troubles.*
> > *They*
> *Delivered the new sink today, and we think you'll*
> *Like it a lot. You turn on the taps and the water*
> *Is just like rain. Yes, it's wet and travels downwards.*

Tonight, the Suffolk County Fire Service are called to deal
With a rubbish fire at the back of the row of houses in which

The Stannard family have their dwelling. It is only a small
Fire, but the loud noise of the appliance outside

Cannot help but disrupt the quiet of their television viewing.
Mr Stannard goes to enquire of the firemen how much longer

They will be. A man on the end of a hose replies, 'Not long.
Quicker if it rains.' And Mr Stannard reflects that it would

Have been better had this fire happened tomorrow, when light
Showers are forecast to fall upon this neck of the woods.

# The Museum of East Anglian Life

No sun blesses the shoulders of the Stannard family
As they traipse moodily The Museum of East Anglian Life:

Abbott's Hall Barn, the domestic displays, Edgar's Farmhouse
And the green field walks, The Boby Building, Alton Watermill,

Grundisburgh Smithy's little reconstructed shed and
What the Stannard family think is a windmill but is in fact

A windpump. Down a specially preserved lane Remus the Suffolk
Punch plods disinterestedly between the shafts of his hay

Cart, looking as happy as the Stannard family feel,
A hulking weight that shrinks them into a relative dimension.

> *You and another walk under the sky*
> *With your thoughts in your own keeping*
> *Extraordinary as earthly folk; no-one*
> *Notices anything spectral about you.*
>
> *Only the edges of history hedge you*
> *With a whisper of doubt as your bulk*
> *Begins to disappear and sounds become*
> *Slightly muted, words losing shape;*
> *Weight and distance are muffled, too.*

We had parked the car in the Market Place and walked the short
Distance to the Museum entrance. A small black cat

Scampered into the hedgerow as we passed by, and on our way
Out it was curled beneath the same hedge, asleep. The sun

Broke through as we drove away, and the traffic lights took
An inordinate time to turn to green.

They did turn, but they took an inordinate long time.
Mrs Stannard said that things happen slowly in East Anglia.

# English as a Foreign Language

Mrs Stannard is asleep and dreaming. She dreams of English
As a foreign language, and that the children have disappeared

Out of her life. The state is one of flux. A removal van
Is loading up outside the house, and she and her husband

Are about to set off to start a new life in a place to which
She does not seem able to give a name. She knows it is somewhere

Post-industrial and near the confluence of two rivers, but even
When she talks to the removal man she does not seem able

To name the place. It is quietly sad without the boys,
But no-one talks about where they are, or why all authority

Is vested in the eminently unsuitable. These are taboo
Subjects, and nobody here ever speaks to the neighbours.

> *Rain drives across England towards Europe;*
> *A cold front whips wind in from the West.*

Mrs Stannard dreams that she and her husband are admiring
Their new house in a place to which she does not seem able

To give a name covered in soot and grime. Cards welcoming
Them to the area were waiting for them when they arrived,

All from people they had never heard of and who wrote
English as a foreign language. Mrs Stannard counts bedrooms

As her husband tries to assemble some comfortable furniture
Using timber oddments he has discovered in the kitchen.

She counts four bedrooms, and realises that there are
No children to put in them. She slumps on the top stair

And cries, and her husband discovers a crowd of Americans
Having a barbecue in the garden. He and his wife cry together.

*Morning comes; the milkman delivers as usual.*

Mr Stannard awakes and does not know where he is; he can hear
Sobbing from outside the room, and he wonders who it was

Made all this dreadful furniture that surrounds him, and
Where on earth the bed he was growing old in has gone.

It is very quiet: it is many years since it was so quiet.
Mrs Stannard awakes to find tears have soaked her pillow.

•

## Another 'Another Day'

Another day,
and the birds are still in the sky
and the sky is still up in the air
and the air is still filled with rumours.

'It is.'                  'It doesn't.'
'It isn't.'              'It does.'

Another day, and holes are still being dug:
       One, a small grave.
       Two, the future out of our hands.
       Three, another small grave.
Another day in a nation of small gardeners.

       Everyman.
       A trowel.

       Heads down.

## 'Parts of the world we want to invade'

and a jacket designed by Metal Box.
It was a dull and damp autumn day
but surprisingly mild for the time of year,
beeswax hanging on the air, your voice
like leaves falling from branches to the grass.
The matter with this world is converging
on the pavement, the footprints
up to your room collecting water, voices
rising from a disregarded television below.
What is falling apart is statement.
On my feet in front of thirty children
or on my back under a double decker bus
I am transported by the idea of travel
into glowing and numerous jungles
and the riotous adventures of the night,
bellows of beasts and love's sharp edge,
the great moment when I take your hand.
Several years ago we would not have been
happy with this life, nor would we
have been satisfied with all we could see.
We would have built tall ships strong
and swallowed oceans in our sleep so
parts of the world would become red.

# A Choice of Wallpaper

Spring and Summer
Lambent Boughs
Squiggles and Dots
After Turner
Green Screen
Lakeland Greys
Toasted Sandwich
Afghan Black
No Smoking Please
Flags of the World
Swings and Roundabouts
Autumn Geometrics
Pink Splendid
Paris
The Flat of the Land
Stormy Waters
Red Alert
Snow on Snow
The Russians Are Coming
Circles and Squares
Various Animals
Stripy
Winter Scenes
Hot Numbers
Manhattan Skyline
Plain White
Available In Other Colours
Eyes
Lambs and Ploughs
Famous Cars
Beethoven and Mozart
After You
Fruit Bowl
Flames
Welsh Memories
Torchlight

Burning Cities
Before Breakfast
Two-Tone
Untitled
Sloping Roofs
Trees with Birds
Déjà Vu
Collage
Industrial Revolution
Black and White
Music Verticals
Lost Love
Relaxation

## Proving Weak and True

Music from a distance can be beautiful,
as can sunsets by the sea and
cottages nestled among green valleys.
Laughter from a playground is pretty nice,
and the happy yapping of dogs.
Reaching the brow of a hill is good,
looking down and tracing the line of the road
as it meanders off into the distance,
and a cool refreshing tumbler of water
can scarcely be bettered.
Bonfire smoke on an early autumn evening
is redolent of nature's robustness,
and a woman wheeling her new baby
along the street is inspiring.
Furry animals are pleasing to children,
and bath-time is especially good
for an archaeologist friend of mine.
Newly-baked bread is a delight,
and even its smell sets the taste buds alight;
bacon has the same effect, and is
probably holy in certain households.
Tears well up in the eyes at the sight
of well-deserved success, and the family
gathered together for a special occasion
should be savoured for what it is.
The scent of flowers filling a room
makes the day, as does a letter
from someone you thought you had lost.
Brilliant colours in dreams are a sign
of affirmation, and a kiss on the cheek
says more than a thousand words.

## One More Brilliant Effect

would be to explode
and take everyone by surprise.
But you could only do that once, I guess,
and then you'd have had your best and only shot.
But tearing the covers off books in anger
is one way, damming the flow of a river
is another possibility, plunging a town into
darkness would be good if they knew it was you did it,
but writing to the paper is a crappy way
of going about things.
Ripping your head off in the market place
would be good if it were raining, eating a dog
to make a point is another way, calling down
a plague of rats from the sky is probably beyond us
these days, but concreting over the oceans
is perhaps still possible if you're quick.
Shouting until your mouth bleeds
is no good, nor is swallowing yourself;
becoming a lightning conductor will draw attention
to your body but not your plight, and remember
animals get more sympathy than people,
usually. Sending the Earth hurtling into the Sun
is almost too big, and stealing the Crown Jewels
would give you more lasting infamy
if they knew it was you did it.

## An Unbelievable Country

Where the gods are silent
Where the prophets are forgotten
Where the heavens are shunned
Where the harvests are locked away
Where the great artists moulder in corners
Where the government is philistine
Where the 19th century never ended
Where the war is still being fought
Where the immigrants remain unwelcome
Where the basic dignities are degraded
Where the old people suffer
Where the air is laced with acid and lead
Where the rivers and streams stagnate greyly
Where the factories pollute entire continents
Where the newspapers trade sex crimes
Where the sex criminals sell newspapers
Where the ships are hardly ever built
Where the roads are always being dug up
Where the children run like animals
Where the trains never run on time
Where the travellers are shunted like swine
Where the weather is getting worse
Where the shops close before you can reach them
Where the policemen do brutality training
Where the work is hard to come by, dear to do
Where the night is rent by screams
Where the people are really stupid

# Madrid

sits in the centre of Spain and wakes up
just as you are falling asleep, like a very old man
who has got out of the habit of taking other people
into consideration. What's the use? he thinks –
they never consider me. Korea, on the other hand,
expects you to take off your shoes before entering
a restaurant; do this, and she will fall in love
with you, and you her, even if it means hobbling
home in the middle of the night in someone else's
sandals.

The Orientals call this 'The Burden of Humour',
which is not what we in the West call anything.

## The Burden of Humour

Like writing a book about mushrooms,
it's undervalued. Like a gasp that becomes
filled with dust, it's not widely appreciated.
Like a smell that looks red but isn't,
it's quite bloody at times. Like a fist
in the mouth, it's contrary. Like a travel
book that refuses to go anywhere, but which
luxuriates on its own patio, it's secure
but quite unheard of. Like a child with
no toys, it's a miserable little sod, and
rightly so. Like the sound of a car
approaching, it's filled with anticipation.
Like the sound of a car going by, it's
realistic, too. Like a lighted window
it's only meaning is at night. Like
a road heading aimlessly into the desert,
it's probably going somewhere. Like a smile
hanging on the air, it's looking for
someone. Like an animal on a leash, it's
always acting hungry. Like one note played
on a cello, it's seeking a social context.
Like a first meeting, it's difficult
to predict. Like a planet, it's very big.
Like an unfinished sentence, it's open
at one end, beckoning the future.

# For Joseph Conrad

From Plymouth in November on *The Wren*
with the dogs to Ponta Delgada;
the dogs could not go ashore.
South-east bearing to Madeira, where
the search for wine proved our ignorance,
if nothing else. Transferred to *Snoopy*,
whose name belied her years, sadly.
In Casablanca, ears at our hotel door
and boys crowding around us in the lanes
were more than Joan could stand. But
the old girl had developed engine trouble,
so we took *The Grand Dame of the Furies*
coast-wise to Essaouira, where a sudden
sand storm whipped up thoughts of
the Foreign Legion, Lloyd Bridges
in a film we saw when we were young.
From there, *Bella Fortuna* drifted
amiably south, port-hopping Africa's
west coast until she rebounded off Dakar
and wound up becalmed in the midst
of the Cape Verde Islands. After
three days, we were picked up by
some Americans in a motor launch
named *Mother Sucker*, and though they
claimed they were headed for Sierra
Leone the sun setting ahead of us
gave their game away. We landed quietly
in Barbados after dark, and sloped off
into the night. In the morning,
*Sunflower* was eager to take us for
a lazy jaunt, which we quite fancied
because the sea was, by now, like land
to us. On terra firma we felt quite sick.
From Barbados to Georgetown, then to
Fortaleza and on to Caravelas, Mar
del Plata and Cape Horn. It was quite

some lazy jaunt. We took up with
thieves about here, and rounded the
Horn under-deck on *The Fred*, playing
cards and drinking stolen gin. They
said the weather was bad outside;
it was pretty rough below, too.
Suddenly a great sleepiness came upon us,
and we awoke to be confronted by
Easter Island disappearing in the distance
behind. The crew had vanished, but
we still had our travellers' cheques.
We smashed into the Pitcairns, and after
some hubbub were placed aboard
*The Dedham Vale* and told never to show
our faces round there again. They
didn't have to say it twice; we were
fast maturing, and the bee-line north
that she cut would have been fine
had the captain taken enough food on
board. In San Francisco it was foggy,
as usual, though that didn't alter
how we ate our way across the city.
A few days later, finding ourselves
wandering aimlessly outside a condo
complex at Oakland we took up with
a couple of guys who were headed
for Vietnam. This was quirky enough
to be too good to miss, so we hopped
aboard *Darkness and Light* and
trusted that someone knew the route.
Someone did know the route, but
nobody knew how to steer the boat;
in New Zealand we cut our losses
and bought berths on *The Cutlass*,
though the mate's eye patch, and hook
where his hand should've been, gave
me nightmares. In Sydney we took
in a quick night at the opera, which

was the first half-decent music we'd
heard for weeks. From there, *Sally D*
made good speed, and we sped past
the Great Barrier Reef like a piece
of piss. The Solomon Islands were
great. It would have been really nice
to stay there longer, but so it goes.
From there to Madras seemed to take
absolutely for ever aboard the rusty
tub *Star of Several Cheap Movies*, which
outside of the dream was actually
the more realistically named *Indian Queen*.
From Madras to Bombay by train (yes,
train – it was cheaper and quicker)
and from there to Djibouti aboard
*The Book of the Dead*. This was one
of our more uneventful trips; and quiet:
nobody said a word the entire journey.
Up the Red Sea, or along it, or through it,
whichever is more correct, on *Sea Horse*,
a pretty good name, and at Suez transferred
to *Elizabeth R*, and the definite smell
of home. Like a bullet across the Med
to Marseille, and some whacky nights
with a language that had us baffled,
and a punchy little trek aboard
*La Belle Dame Sans Chemise* to Gibraltar,
which we thought was worth a shot
or two. We were right, as it happens.
Hopped up the Iberian coast with
*Lady Orange, Happy Days*
rescuing us from a beer binge in Bordeaux
with some English students who were
a disgrace to our race. Docked at Falmouth
on a wet and windy Monday morning
before the shops were open.

## A New Life

Sat here under the night
I can feel your breath
on my neck, and it's cold.
This new life's okay, I guess,
and I shouldn't complain.
Rupert phones, and we
have a chuckle about some
little thing that's funny
to us, and it's good.
Upstairs, the kids are
in bed waiting for me
to kiss them goodnight.
It's cosy up there.
I've shut out all
the draughts, and painted
the walls in warm colours.
Goodnight, kids. Have
some really good dreams.

# Heroes and Heroines

Any changes we make will be small
    and barely worth the time or effort;
and who will know the difference,
    and who will care? All this reminds
me of a very long short story in which
    the hero and the heroine spend all
their time hunting madly for any sign
    of a plot. Eventually, they stumble
upon a blank page, and what lives they had
    come to an abrupt end. You put
the book down and look around the room
    for something to eat. But you see
nothing, though you can hear a great deal.
    The police sirens rip through the city,
breaking glass plays its brief music on
    the air, booted feet grind the gravel
outside the back window. Footsteps!
    But what is there to be afraid of –
we know how safe the world is,
    everybody loves us, and nobody
covets all our expensive electrical gear:
    in short, it's a wonderful world,
and if somebody wants to walk round
    the back of our house in the middle
of the night it's certainly for our
    own good. This reminds us of
childhood, how the hero and the heroine
    were floundering around looking for
an explanation of life's mysteries,
    and all they can get out of anyone
is how it's all for their own good,
    that explanations only serve to
confound the issue. So when it came
    to looking for a job, or for someone
to hitch up with for the rest of their lives,
    it was all so random, and conducted

with such an air of dull ignorance,
    that a disaster was bound to happen.
It did. But not immediately. It was
    like waiting for a bus in some ways –
you knew the wait would be long and tedious
    and filled with great swathes of doubt,
and you knew also that when the bus arrived
    it would be necessary to haul your whole
body aboard, even though – when it came
    to the crunch – a little bit of you
thought better of it, and another littler
    and weaker bit of you wanted
strenuously to do the magical thing and
    pack off in the opposite direction.
It was over in that part of the world
    where golden spires touched the blue
sky and sunlight glinted off stained
    glass windows decorated by
the laughter of children that fiction
    and wonderment had their home;
but where you were headed lived small men
    with small minds, and architecture
that demonstrated how far away from
    common sense, aesthetics, and
the rights of man they had travelled.
    Getting on with people was tough here,
everything turned into a competition;
    if you weren't born a gladiator or
a confidence man it was always
    going to be an uphill struggle. And
then there was love, a serial where
    the hero and the heroine slobbered
fruitlessly with one another through
    a random series of costume changes,
hotel bedrooms, and family dinners
    before scuttling away into an imagined sun-
set to, if not live happily ever after,
    at least share the burden of debt

that had been granted them with glee
    by their parents – grim people who
had stayed together all these years because
    their imaginations could not stretch
to another, different life. Nothing was easy.
    Everywhere you looked problems loomed,
their ugly heads peeking above the dark
    parapet of the future. Industries
foundered, poverty flourished, the cement
    holding society together cracked
seriously, and even the world, which we
    had come to love through years of
watching nature documentaries on TV,
    began to fall apart. In the middle
of all that, which when listed (albeit
    briefly) is enough to piss even
the most devout of optimists severely off,
    one is reminded of the legend (which
has its basis in fact, though its most
    famous version is rooted in European
folk-tale, taken by boat to the Americas
    and there turned into a classic of
transcendentalist literature, and now easily
    available in a moderately priced
book of the film) of the man and woman who
    dug a hole in the middle of their
village and, after chucking a load of food
    and supplies into it, clambered down
themselves, and persuaded onlookers to
    shovel earth into the hole on top
of them. They were buried alive! But later,
    much later, when the Town Council
after much debate ordered they be dug up
    and given a decent burial, and
workmen with shovels and spades bore
    down to find them, what did
they discover but a happy family with
    smiles that lit up the dark cavern;

small children, naked but radiant,
    abounded. True, the food was nearly
run out, but the narrative skips over that
    and emphasises the metaphorical nature
of the tale. There's a hell of a moral
    in there somewhere, too, if you can
be bothered to look for it; actually,
    in this age of dirty realism, it's
not metaphors or morals we're after,
    but clarification of the evidence.
But that's another story. In this one,
    the one we wake up to every day,
the hero and the heroine wallow
    in a jolly time among friends who
are also happy to be alive and to be
    always confronted by life's bounties.
They are all very nauseating people,
    with too much money for their own
good, and a new car parked outside
    that has poor taste written all over
it. They spend a lot of time in expensive
    restaurants showing off their bad
manners, and talk too loudly, just so
    everybody knows how overloaded
with garbage they are. But the trouble
    is, so many people are actually
impressed by their behaviour that
    the world speeds up on its down-
ward spiral, and for the few who don't
    like the look of what's going on
even The Bible, for God's sake, begins
    to take on a sense and sensibility
that hitherto had been unregarded.
    But we should avoid that particular
track, because the hero and the heroine
    of that famous opening chapter
have no clothes on, and this is not
    that sort of text. In fact, it's

the sort of text that reminds us of an
        epic of the 22nd century, where
even the idea of the epic is symbolic of
        a supreme optimism we can't, quite
honestly, sustain. But it's good to
        look on the bright side, and
finally we are reminded of a novel
        in which the hero and the heroine
are found one day in an idyllic setting
        somewhere deep in the English
countryside. She is perched on a farm
        gate; he stands chewing idly
on a long stem of grass. In the back-
        ground a herd of disinterested
cows chew the cud, and above them
        an occasional fluffy cloud
scuds across an otherwise clear blue
        sky. They are discussing some
little nothing, the sort of thing which
        has occupied the minds of lovers
since the year dot. They are happier
        than they thought possible
or even morally justifiable. Suddenly,
        just as they embark on a more
serious chat about whether or not they
        will be able to afford a fitted
kitchen when they are married,
        the unthinkable happens: yes,
their little corner of England takes
        the brunt of a nuclear attack
and we will never know what sort of
        kitchen destiny had in store
for them. They are cut off in the prime
        of their promising lives
and we are left to curse the novelist
        for being such a bastard.
But this is the artist's great joy –
        balancing all creation in

the palm of his hand and knowing
    all the answers; or, if
that fails, at least having the chance
    to call the whole tacky show
off. Which is usually the best thing,
    and the only decent way.

## Optimism and Despair

There are a few things we must think about, a few things
That have to do with the unenviable future of mankind.
I mean, look at The Ice Age and how it begins:

Snow accumulates in a man's life and trouble starts.
There was nothing but a slight drizzle of rain, and suddenly
He's in a drift, up to his neck in problems and aching hearts.

He is expected to know how to cope, and how to bear
The Winter. It is assumed he knows all about hierarchies:
He is watching a TV movie called 'If I Had A Million' where

A department store Santa Claus believes he is the real
Mr. Claus. Then he switches channels and gets
'The Ragpicker', the tragic story of an illegal

Immigrant who gets involved with a wealthy Texas family.
And the two movies are identical. They have the same stars
And they are telling the same story, of the poor and wealthy.

The difficulty concentrates when we realise that we
Are only bewildered spectators. We are not participating.
Take Nature. Take, for example, this splendid tree:

Can you name it and say what kind it is? Root and branch are
A part of your life, but which of us is able to name
The important parts of our lives? Do we know them? And mar-

Vellous and more vital snippets of information are blowing
Around like dust on the breeze than we shall ever know, but it
Is like China, immense and lonely, and we're afraid of knowing.

We are scared of love, the way it grows from an unseen seed,
Only to go mad and crazy and then wither and die
As we sit in familiarity and watch each other bleed.

There is always some smart analogy to be drawn. Imagine
The ocean, kissing shorelines as it follows the Moon
From one day to the next. There is a certain pleasure in

It. And there is a certain peace and adventure in it too,
Neither of which is it given to many of us to experience.
What we try for sometimes is to conquer it, or to

Entrap it for our own dim purposes, the details of which we say
We will work out later, when the time is right and
We have the leisure to read the manual before we play

The game. But a cloud hangs over a divided nation,
And something crusty dries upon our tourist tongues
In one flying moment of supreme and inspiring consternation

That'll stop us ever again dismissing little things: dreams
And peas, for instance. Trouble is, we forget the unforgettable
As readily: there's always a reason to push it aside, it seems.

Here come the reinforced battalions of the new 1987 Police
Armed for a violent and intense struggle, riot and mayhem. And
Here's a competition: describe this uneasy Western peace.

It's always the thought of losing what we have that holds us
Down as though bound and gagged: old anoraks are pleasing,
So are famous people. And famous people enjoy being famous!

What's the point in being famous if your ego doesn't grow to
Almost explode with the extravagant ecstasy of it?
Is that the sound of an animal orgasm I am hearing from you?

I am in the factory canteen and someone asks me,
How is the new bed? and I reply that the bed is okay it's
The interminable headaches I can't tolerate. Yes, ecstasy

Is a rare enough thing and feeling sort of grey and low-
Key is the mean and common denominator that unites us.
All those fish in the oceans, all those animals go-

Ing around their kingdoms, and only we reserve the right
To be always complaining. One day we shall reflect on all this
Using a photo album and jottings made in a day book at night:

It's us, you, we and I, in a window booth at The Happy Eater,
And the list of things bothering us is getting longer all
The time. Three of us are squeezed on to a two-seater

Bench and this morning we woke up unaware (see us brushing
A light flaking of snow from the bed covers) that all night
During our nervous sleep an anger had been brewing.

Gosh, how annoying people can be at breakfast, munching loud
As pigs and soiling the brand new newspaper with milk and jam.
They are in such a rush to be out at work and with the crowd!

Meanwhile, this nuclear family in The Happy Eater enjoys
(Have you ever thought how misused words often are?) a sad
Little meal and the sullen service of a waitress who annoys

Us and has dry skin all over her face and her forearms.
Even gorillas get fed hygienically, and look at her! She is
Flaking into our cereal bowls. Sound the alarms!

Such horrors prevent us from looking out of the window: we stop
To gaze at the prints on the wall in their lurid frames,
We admire our reflection in the window of every other shop

We pass on our way to the bus station, or to the food store.
Our hair is all wrong! Our clothes are already old-fashioned!
If only we were furry, and free of all this! But before

Lunch we realise, queuing for the auto-teller at the bank,
That as a race we have spent millions of years learning how to
Talk and write just so we can complain about things, or thank

The government for giving us a job. Pity the poor dumb
Animals who are quite happy save for the threat of extinction
That is all our doing. Smarter than them? I go numb

Because of this state of affairs. Humans! We have invented
Great machines to do great things, and still soluble aspirin
Refuses to dissolve completely. So much happens and is resented

That it is all but impossible to see anything clearly. I mean,
Here comes the doctor, waving a prescription pad, telling us
It's the strain keeping us on edge. On edge! I've been

On this fucking precipice all my life, and still can't name the sea
My feet are dangling above, still I am confounded by the ships
That float past full of people who look as confused as me.

A cold wind blows, and from this disadvantage point it appears
That what we are all in our own way trying to steer clear of
Is that huge problem that is at the root of all our fears:

Why am I such a mess? Is it because of how my mother treated
Me, something she did that screwed me up? Or am I a mess
Because of some awful and plain wrong decisions which defeated

Me at some stage of my life? Or do I blame history
(Time caught and stuck between book covers) for placing you and
I here where we can do nothing about the state we

Are in? An interruption interrupts the flow: WAIT! HOLD BACK!
I think things are not so grim as this chap is making out, so
Hang on a second before you go on along this depressing track!

Yesterday my wife and I stood on the cliff top looking sea-
Ward, and denied that we were in any sort of mess. A few
Problems, minor skirmishes in the day before night, seem to be

A part of a necessary mix. Optimism and despair
Exist in a disconcerting equilibrium. This is ordinary. Things
Aren't great, but won't get better if we sit around wear-

Ing our mope masks all day. What the heck! I do a lot
Of unwise things, some of which I know are bad for me but
Others are so wacky that whether they are bad for me or not

Doesn't matter. 'You just go on your nerve', learn the tricks.
It's like the relationship between a fellow and his car,
Blessèd harmony and downright antagonism in a mix

That works. And even if the paintwork is marked
The most important thing is getting from A to B in one piece,
It seems to me, and to be sober and industrious. But parked,

Nothing is simple, or as simple as you might wish.
You hear the music of flowers that children have been
Instructed to describe and freeze for ever in their English

Books. But if this is music it is not from this planet,
Or is it from this planet after all? Is it even music? The fog
Descends and surrounds us as we attempt to understand it.

Meanwhile, Pete is marking his record and cassette decks
With infra-red ink to foil burglars on dark nights when
We are out and having fun with members of the opposite sex.

He also marks the video, the cameras, the television,
The PC, his electric typewriter and Anne's Beatles albums with
This marker he bought from a doorstep salesman whose position

Seemed to be enviable. He could've sold him the North Sea:
Pete's one of those people who do things then think about them:
A real animal when it comes to sex, a darling in the laundry.

But what about God? How long is it since you imagined a hun-
Dred new colours in which to clothe your children?
Let's say this: We should be new under the sun

And even if we don't think so, we have left that stuff
To God for so long that we fail to notice the possibilities.
And we feel in some vague way that we have had enough.

Here comes the snow: in 1952 everything was warm and new,
And you and we and I knew that it was never going to be our job
To explain how structures work and are constructed, or to

Show how we stumble upon meaning with our eyes taped shut
And our wits slumbering on the pillow. No, it wasn't that.
You and we and I were not those sort of people. But

Here's the snow: we discover at a certain stage that some
Of the world is made of glass and our friends have broken
Their mouths. They spend most of their time cooking at home,

Or examining the sheets of friends, and skin tones, and the way
In which snow really is a method of keeping babies outside
Until they are needed. Then one winter's day

We find their bodies have turned into trees. In the morning,
White, a hand hovers over the snooze button of the clock radio
At the bedside, and politics mixes with sport and a warning

Of Soviet aggression. Someone has invented a fruit that'll make
Getting up and going to the factory seem wonderful. Suddenly
It's like being in love for the first time, for God's sake!

But you should pay more attention to this fleeting
And mysterious feeling, that's for sure. It's a good 'un, and
The money you bring home doesn't get near it, as when meeting

A child he gives you a short poem written at school:

> 'In a cavern in the snow,
> As lovely as could be,
> There are lots of icicles
> And a bumblebee.
> Then along come children
> In their autumn coats
> Then down come some snowflakes.
> All the children laughed
> And giggled in their play.
> Everyone was happy
> The very first winter day!'

And you, big grown up, mutter into your concrete and
Fashionable sleeve, 'How sweet and naïve, the little fool!'

This was you and I and we and us back in 1959, when shoes
Were sensible and we knew what barbers were for! When TV shows
Starred The Beverley Sisters and we went to bed before The News;

It was like being half alive. Now it is like being half dead.
This is the first line of the funniest joke in the world,
But I keep the second line hidden inside my head.

There is a gag, I'm sure there is. But lately my luck
Has changed: a great clatter of engines and groaning of wheels
And steel rods and stuff like that has taken over. Yuk!

How many times, here beneath the satellites' glow,
Have we sat together and warmed our blood talking about coal?
Coal: where it comes from and where it ought to go.

There is in this country a disturbing and re-occuring
Passion: you wake up in the morning half wanting to run out
Into the street in your Dream Boy nightshirt to yell something

Mad and rude so the neighbours notice you; but you don't,
And I don't, and none of us ever do, and we share the bitter-
Ness and regret, not knowing if it's true that we won't

End yet, that its hardly begun. And in the afternoon
At about four someone who looks a lot like me writes a page or
Two of a great picaresque novel that will soon

Be finished. 'Here I Go Again' is thick on intent and thin
On plot as yet but the mystery of it all is the kick. Yes,
I don't know where I'm going, or where it is we've been.

The other person's way of life often remains a mystery to us,
Standing here like stones, analysing the spaces between blades
Of grass, inventing the telescope, catching a bus

To the shops with someone very much like us. I've worked out
That with no money or charisma I'm not going to alter the case
Much, so what the hell: make me happy, make me shout

With joy! Several things we thought implausible and impossible
Are happening as we sit here dipping our lips  in white spirit.
Your life has become a crime with a motive that's debatable

And my career is becoming ever more difficult to un-
Derstand as the days turn from russet to ice to bud green
Again. I thought I was the nurse, the hospital and the sun,

But there are no more miracles, and there are very few
Excuses as people drive past in their luxuries, eyeing
Themselves and their new hairstyles in the rear-view

Mirrors. I wave my arms, but they crash anyway. Yes,
Men dig up the trees, women re-plant them; dinners get cooked
And moods get thrown about how it's all such a mess.

Down the road a little way, an old lady bursts into tears
Because she is so alone in the world, and you and I send our
Children in to her as a weak gesture of compassion. The year's

1986, and people still cry for fear and solitude and sadness.
The sky remains fixed over our heads for night to come and bury
Us again in a comfortless and cowering blindness.

I'm getting angry, and the thought of how politics must play
A part in all of this is swelling up behind these lines. But
That's another story, or the same story told on another day.

Tomorrow the sun will come up from behind the factory
And some opportunities will be with it, and some threats, too.
On the bedclothes, a trace of snow. The factory is empty.

## Signs of Greatness #9

Goths or Vandals are gnawing at the city's borders
and you say, I am suffering so much anxiety,
I don't recognise all these people who act like tourists,
and my baby is growing up and refuses to open her eyes.
I know what you mean: it's a state of siege.
You're not quite sure what it is you're up against but
everything you cherish seems to be falling off the world.

I think one sign of greatness is within the brick,
able to be a part of the wall, and happy as well
to be still and secure in its own solidity.
My father was a brick. And I can remember him
speaking of his father who, he said, was a real brick.
I grew up hoping one day to be a brick also,
but here we are, and you know how it's all turned out.

## *Signs of Greatness #10*

It's less than two days to the big day, and Europe's guns
are primed as they should be, and they're even aimed in
the right direction. People are preparing to be ever so brave.
The intelligensia are having one last quick read.

I think one sign of greatness is to be able to own up
to cowardice when all about you are busily showing off how
tough and fearless they are able and happy to be.
A man with caterpillar tracks across his torso, a professor
of tough shit, tells you that it's iron filings for tea
and from now on you're going to have to horde your excrement
so the country will smell so awful the enemy will think twice
before invading. That's a tremendous ruse, you say. A genius
must've thought that one up. A man with razor blades the length
of his spine says, Yeah, it's great. It's gunna be Paradise.

## Signs of Greatness #13

My neighbours sleep blinkered but with their ears to the wall
and the Kingdom, whittled away by time and the tide of events,
is full of people so like them that it's impossible to relax.
If you hadn't noticed, the bastards are still in control.
Whilst hanging new net curtains in the parlour window yesterday
I espied patrolling down the carriageway a constable mounted
on a snow white charger, and in his hand was a small tree:
if you did not know any better, you'd say it was natural.

I think one sign of greatness is to know your country,
to be able to speak freely about its condition
and not be intimidated when some out-dated creed is invoked
as they try to tie your tongue up in the knots of patriotism.
When people say we should remember the 'Great' you know what
to say: 'The bastards, my dear, are still in control.'

# From *The Heart of Stone*

You say you are over the moon
but I know you're just over your mum's;
nothing you can do will twist my arm
or force me to say, 'I love her
and we're going up in the world.î'
Rather, 'I love her but it's
killing me aesthetically.'
Certainly I remember
how the evening sun illumined
the estuary as we strolled complacently
during The Age of Discovery,
but times are changed and
though we wear the cloak of decency
we know how much is corrupt.
People are taking to the streets
and you can't blame them:
I'm almost ashamed of our coffee table
and the books we scatter on it;
I am embarrassed by two girls
carrying an anvil between them, and
a child weighed down by climbing gear.

# Thinking of the Sea

## 1. The Dangerous Sea

Timothy came home wet. It was a hot sunny day.
I said something almost too clever about
how some people contrive their own weather.

The sea, said Timothy, stood up on its hind legs
and would've picked up the entire town in its arms
if it hadn't been for

## 2. The Driving Sea

Diana was in bed with Sea-Fever. It was a hot sunny day.
From across the quiet road the sound of a man tinkering
with a hammer at the engine of a Rover came.

There are people in Barnsley who have never seen
a grey mist on the sea's face and a grey dawn breaking.
Speaking of which, John Masefield once spoke of

## 3. The Possible Sea

Oceans began with frogs, said Andrew. It was a hot sunny day.
Then they became the seas as we know them, and frogs
trundled inland to live in ponds and quiet pools.

Everything starts somewhere. If there are things at
the bottom of which we know nothing then perhaps this is
a beginning also. And to discover something new is like

## 4. The Sleeping Sea

Timothy came into our room. It was a hot sunny day.
He said he could hear the snoring of the sleeping sea.
We listened. It was true. You could discern pyjamas also.

And when it got dark, the sea awoke and began to sing.
Full soon an immense choir struck up a chorus,
so it was impossible to dream. Realism is defined as

*5. The North Sea*

## The Detective

            unless it rained. Then
we were going to wander until,
under cover of night, stealth
would bring us to the door.

Lying there. An open book
at the bedside with a pencil
snug in the cleft of the pages.

Dressing clumsily, breeze
disturbing the curtains,
took longer than intended,
running the risk of discovery.

'The streets are not a good place.'
Things must be said, come what may:
decisions have to be made.

But the son's honesty.
Tomorrow we would notice calmly
the sun, and how it rises
to reveal our deceptions.

Unless it rained. And then
speaking on tiptoe she says,
You forgot this. Handing me it.

Did he? The detective

## Phil's Poem

I've decided to be nice to everyone
and not tell any more lies;
but with the sun shining on this brilliant
November evening I have to go into some family history
before things can even begin to come clear –
Stannards have never been possessed of the pioneer spirit,
they have never stood at the edge of the prairie
and seen a little chunk of it in their mind's eye
and wanted to make it their own,
they have never saluted the star-spangled banner,
and they have never been called Phil. What's more,
Stannards have never been famous, they have never
stood out in a crowd, they have never been mentioned
in dispatches, they have never contributed much
to debates, charities, culture or suggestion boxes,
they have never been rich, they have never
been slung in jail, they have never lusted openly
but kept it to themselves (like smoke), they have
never learnt to swim, not even when their heads
were being held under water, they have never marched,
struck, protested, demonstrated or complained,
they have never shed light on the darkness,
they have never spoken what was on their minds
because they have never had much on their minds
worth speaking of, they have never cared much
for style, or suffering if that suffering was
more than an arm's length distant, and they have never
been missed after they were gone, because
they have never been noticed while they were there.
Some things can, perhaps, now become clear.

## People are Dying in the Sun

But there is nothing in the world
we want to do about the wrong things.
We're not here. We're there:
on the other side of the enormous bed
a man impersonates a pig,
his face a notice-board from which all information
                has been stripped:
health warnings, the social calendar, job opportunities –
it's all nothing in the world.
Only the sun. Impersonally shining.
It burns the side of your face
through the car window; it dries the ink of this poem
                hurriedly.
And this must be gone soon, before too much is said.
When too much is said, too much is regretted.

## The Life

The book is open
at page 1038
It's been a very busy life
full of people and things and difficult ideas
but I've enjoyed food, and often
someone has been here to enjoy it with me
Pleasures have been various
Work has been rewarding
It's been nice
and my brain is teeming with the names of friends
who've graced my days: Ben Tom Audrey and Jane
That's only four; there were loads more
And I'm glad I wasn't born a leper in a hot country
or a street urchin in a hot country
It's been good to be English
It was an easy language to learn
and I liked the clothes
And I liked the freedom
There was always something new to explore:
once we went to Exmouth
and stayed a whole hour
It was nice
England
It's been really nice
It has
I'll be sorry to see it go

## The Slightest Effort

The slightest effort is a waste of time
but you have to keep your chin up, otherwise
the world would shrink uncontrollably
defying all the laws of physics but fulfilling
every terrible threat each bad dream posed.
Outsiders cannot understand, but
first-hand knowledge of how the game goes
is all you need to foresee the result;
everything is phoney and nothing's real,
and there's nobody anywhere you can trust.
All your belongings are worth nothing,
and the house you were a child in has gone;
when you walk around there now all you can do
is smell your memories and taste their salt.
It's all over, and the past can't be caught
and re-lived or caressed or re-organised.
You were told it was going to be
an up-hill struggle, and it's been steeper
than probably even they imagined it to be:
they had jobs but were poorly paid;
you had a job but now you don't have one.
They had a future which was probably
going to closely resemble their past;
if you have a future, it's difficult to see
and impossible to know how it will be.

# Three Days

*1.*

I shall have to be masculine and strong,
as usual; I am walking on air,
but every so often get this really exhausted feeling
in my bones. The soporific routine of these days
filled with inedible food and fancy gadgets
trips on along, and I think about placing
my palm on the hot iron, but never do it.
Here comes yet another breath
            that's not going to be a song.


*2.*

And here comes the story of the lion who opened
his mouth during a dream of fruit and an entire circus
was found to be living in the red wet red of his gums.
His was the bite filled with jugglers and clowns
and a beautiful girl riding
            bareback under the stars.


*3.*

It's another heavy day and I am sipping my Earl Grey,
about to be knocked out (though I don't know it)
by a volume of poems
            about love affairs and trains.

## Painting the Day

Here once again is the blue sky,
　　and its friend the big river.
Over there are the cows in a field,
　　and a train is speeding along
the embankment on its way to the city.
　　In the blue sky a pattern
of clouds is pushed lazily by a breeze
　　that's gentle as a child's breath;
on the big river a little boat bobs
　　about, and a man sits fishing
quietly, puffing at a pipe and thinking
　　private thoughts. In the field,
the cows check their bodies and
　　see that it's getting near milking
time; a little girl on the train
　　peers out of the grimy window
and into the smoke belching out
　　of the factory in the distance,
beyond the dark grey ribbon
　　of the river. The fisherman
feels peckish, and gets out the packed
　　lunch his wife made for him
at breakfast time; he hasn't had a bite
　　all morning. In the blue sky
an arrowhead of geese flies picturesquely
　　away from the sun, and a kite
flown by a small boy in a green meadow
　　flaunts its colours at the air.
An overblown motor launch bears up river,
　　and its swell throws the little
boat of the fisherman this way and that,
　　spilling the man's tea. The train
is long gone, and a factory hooter goes
　　also. Down river, just around
a bend, a grey-green effluent seeps
　　into the water from a waste pipe

secreted in the bank on the factory side,
    and further down river amid
a whitey-grey sludge that floats on
    the surface are a lot of dead fish.
A few dark clouds appear on the horizon
    and the river becomes increasingly
agitated as the breeze stiffens and
    has to be redefined as a wind.
The boy with the kite goes home, and
    the fisherman rows ashore,
muttering to himself that the river
    isn't what it used to be.

## Kitchen

I think, said Mr Gleam (the polish to get your house clean),
that we should scrub out all our miserable childhoods
from the book each of us has in him or her. That'll do it,
and it's a great way, said Mr Bark (the all-meat dog dinner),

of letting the world off the hook, too. Not that
the world deserves it, he added, sticking his reputation
above the parapet of controversy. I know what you mean,
chipped in Mr Whipp (the top topping). It's too easy to be

conciliatory when you're left to languish in a cupboard
all day but we mustn't soften up. No problem, said Mr Bio
(more than a bleach, with the smell of spring winds).

As soon as you mention love, beauty, forgiveness and
freedom of speech I'll be there to remind you that
everything comes down to just one thing in the end.

Upon which the kitchen became very quiet, like thought,
and the sun streamed in through the window to hit the oven.

## When Danger Threatens

It is very pleasant to be thought of as beautiful.
Words which come to mind at the same time as you
include 'pavilion', 'balm' and 'shilling'; also,
at the end of your road there is a tumbledown house
outside which kids stand huddled in small knots
whispering about their secrets and other kids.
It's okay to stroll past them as they do this, but
to care about what they think of you is a mistake.
Crossing the great sea in an airplane several
months later, you find yourself thinking about them
as you look down into nothing from nothing,
and you wonder if it was them or what they mean
that made you decide to sell up and leave home.
Words which flit into your mind at this time
and which flit just as quickly out of it again
include 'spanner', 'highway' and 'scheme'; also,
the pain in your head that you could never describe
with any degree of accuracy comes on again,
and you realise it's like a colossal pair of boots
behind your eyes, and a good word is 'brick'.
And yes, it is very pleasing to be considered
beautiful, which is probably something the sun
mutters to itself every day as it sinks slowly into
the ocean, as it is doing now, and as it does
with such grace every day for those who will see.

# The Wind Getting Up

The sky coming crashing down is bothersome:
you don't expect that kind of thing to fall
on you without warning. That's what you
pay your taxes for, why you take home less
than you earn, why you can't afford to eat.
The house you built with your own hands
is not much to look at, but it's still
more than a pile of bricks against the wind.
The outside has just been painted by a man
you met in a pub, and it looks nicely spruced.
Inside, each room is stamped with character
thoroughly English and sure of itself:
not exactly cheap, but even you would not
claim it to be sumptuous. Moderate. Perhaps
moderate is the best word. But it's not how
you would speak of this latest disaster,
the great grey air coming down on your life
just when you thought it was safe to relax –
if not for the rest of your days at least
for a bit. It goes to show you can't be less
than vigilant for a moment. You close your
eyes and the world disappears; there's always
a thief behind you, or an accident waiting on
the wings of the wind for a moment to happen.

## Another Gift

comes handed reluctantly down from on high,
and it's crying. Quiet ones are best,
but only come into their own on their own.
Uniforms are worn by people with no hearts,
it says in the manual, and to give is
more pleasing than to receive, apparently.
On the Tuesday before Christmas (wet
and windy they said it was going to be,
though it turned out calm and surprisingly
mild for the time of year, which just goes
to show) another gift arrives in the mail:
something pleasant from somewhere nice?
Or something ugly from somewhere ugly?
Urban presents have a habit of bursting
into flames when you are least expecting
a fire in your life, and men in balaclavas
can sometimes have mischief in their
minds, and deadly weapons up their sleeves.
Some men want to give that gift which
nobody particularly wants to receive,
though many have things thrust upon them.
Good days arrive unbidden, as do bad,
but what the future holds is not for us
to know beyond the fact that night follows
day as sure as children are a delight,
gifts with which the fortunate are blessed.

## A Few Words of Wisdom

If the kestrel sits quietly looking at the air it's a sign that change is imminent. Smoke goes down the cottage chimney, and the world is turned irrevocably on its head. Now, when you awaken into morning's gloom and the afternoons are pared back by an early falling darkness, the one thing (among a million others, actually) that is so difficult is imagining anything different. Even after a splendid dream that had you waking up in a really good and unusual mood there are limits on exuberance.

Living in a particular place on a map does not necessarily mean you know where you are. Speaking a specific language does not mean you know what you are saying, or what you are talking about. Breathing in and out at irregular intervals does not mean you are alive.

# The Salute

The fat man takes his hat off to the slim volume
of verse written by some anonymity from Europe,
and wedges his window open to let in some fresh air.
The breeze kisses the crowd of sightseers on the lips,
and then travels untainted but changed to the sea,
where a new life awaits those who will take risks.
Meanwhile, when the shopping precinct opens,
the radio celebrity waves to the few fans who are
braving the cold, and a few of those fans wave
back and mouth lusting obscenities in his direction.
The fat man, incidentally, has fallen asleep with
a greeting on his tongue in a foreign language.
In a book, a peasant girl whose name is immaterial
(a very strange name for a girl, though not for a boy)
is shown curtseying to a King and Queen as if
her life depended on it, which it probably does.
In the same book, a strapping young fellow-me-lad
drinks to living life hard and fast before going out
to be pierced through the heart by a duellist's rapier.
If you pay a compliment to a chef in a classy café
a child may misquote you as having said, 'Condiments
to the chef!' and a comic on stage at The Hippodrome
will take a bow as applause rings in his ears after
a particularly smutty joke about a building society.
An accolade, according to the dictionary, is to do
with the bestowing of a knighthood, but saying 'Well
done, here's sixpence' is a version of it also.
One should pay homage to one's masters, and poets
must recognise that Shakespeare is the real boss,
whoever the hell he was or whoever he turns out to be.
One should not, however, scrape around at the heels
of scrimping little toadies who merely pretend
to be important; hob-nobbing with these parasites
is the worst form of behaviour after usury. Finally,
a quick knee-bend to the glorious angels and God's
marvellous kingdom won't do any harm, though probably
he'll know if you're sincere or just trying it on.

# The Statue We Made

Her feet touch lightly the golden sand,
and her hair brushes the sky and its clouds;
we made her that way, after much debate.
She is clothed in a tunic of grey stone
that reflects the spectrum and is always
changing hue. It is never grey, and it never
looks or feels like stone. In one hand she
holds a book of fairy stories; this takes
the place of a holy book which was deemed
wholly inappropriate considering our history.
The other hand is bandaged, a symbol of
our people's lasting wound: lest we forget.
She stands with one leg slightly shorter
than the other: this gives her an aspect
of leaning, which we thought might indicate
that we have learned something about
compromise, and seeing the other man's
point of view. Some thought this too subtle,
but she leans anyway. Many arguments raged
long into our long nights about her body,
whether she should be curvy and sexual or
more the muscular type. This was an awful
difficult area of debate, considering
that sexuality is (like poetry) in the eye
of the beholder. But populism prevailed,
and she is quite shapely, but not so she
inflames the lusty imaginations of young
men or the jealousies of our womenfolk.
On her lips is the faintest trace of a smile,
but sometimes this appears sad and wan
rather than cheery. In some lights
it looks like a smirk, but more often one
gets the sense that it is a smile borne
of tears and the most immense of regrets.
Her cheeks glow, especially as they catch
the ember rays of the setting sun. We made

her eyes shine brightly, but it could be
with anger or delight. It is impossible
to say which, though some think it both.
She stands in such a place that travellers
see her huge silhouette in dreams, days
before they step into her gigantic shadow.

# A Crescent

moon hangs above the row of houses opposite
and we have been selecting wallpaper
from a book almost too heavy for me to lift.
I would, you say, like the walls to say something.
I hope, I said, they say what they think.

The girl over the road's boyfriend gets
on his moped and tries in vain to start it up.
She stands in the doorway but it's too dark
to see her face; he is kicking like a fiend,
and suddenly the machinery whisks him away into
a night poorly illumined by elderly streetlamps.

We listen to the quiet deepening where earlier
the Salvation Army band imposed its music on us.
I would, you say, very much have liked to be taller
and slimmer and commanded a band of warriors
that trawled the world collecting treasures
beyond even the wildest of my dreams.

I look at your head on the pillow, but
it's dark and I can't make out your expression
though I imagine it to be one of utter sublimity.
I hope, I say, that we can afford that wallpaper.
I don't, you say, like you with a beard.
I won't always have one, I say. Things change,
and our lives won't always be like this.

## Our Glory

Here's a box of delights, but sometimes I think
I'm too old to open it. Other times I figure I'm not
only too old, but it's probably against the law.
And then I know for sure that even if it's not
against the law then someone somewhere will raise
an objection because certain people are born
with a mission to object, and they delight in
fulfilling it. Here's a desert, and all it is
is sand, seeming endless miles of it, the only
punctuation a few haphazard camels dotted about
for no apparent purpose. Occasionally a wind blows
and moves the sand about a bit, but it's pretty
pointless. Suddenly a tree springs up out of nowhere,
and on it is blossom, of glorious colours. At once
the desert is a different place: the world is
changed for ever. But here comes someone: he
objects to the tree because it's casting a shadow.

## Slow Asleep

The water is coming in through the roof
of the world, and not being swimmers we shall surely
drown, but

'when our days do end they are not done;
and though we die, we shall not perish quite,
but live two lives, where others have but one.'

Granted, I may be dreaming, but 'this sacred art'
keeps me fast awake at night, thinking.

Demons. Angels.

# The Swimmers

As one cast head-first by cruel Fate into a terrible quagmire
and left to flounder half-submerged with his feet sticking heavenward,
and who is hauled to safety on the end of a silvery rope
let down and looped about his ankles by a mysterious stranger
astride a wingèd horse, and who after he is dried off and dusted down
by his mother tries to tell his remarkable story to anyone who will listen
but nobody will, my evenings are spent cleaning these fragile ornaments,
each of which represents an emotion, their appearance distorted
by the weird light that falls upon them and that seems to emanate
from my eyes ever since the night the darkness was rent by a voice
like the sound a mountain makes when it moves a few paces off its spot,
and pigeons, or perhaps they were doves, fluttered around my head
as a reminder that even when we feel most lost and abandoned by everything
there is a fixed point in the universe we can latch on to, as when
two swimmers swimming together across an enormous stretch of water
begin to feel that they have lost their way and must surely die of exhaustion,
never reaching the shoreline for which they set out with their hearts full
of enthusiasm and hope, and confident of their own strengths,
and one hears 'the bubbling cry of some strong swimmer in his agony'
while the other hears the unmistakable happiness of a brass band,
and then a police car's siren, but for a horrifying moment or two
cannot tell from which direction they come, these sounds of life,
and a bird is silhouetted on the wing against the fiery Sun above,
and you wonder if there is ever any relief from this sense of being
two swimmers swimming together across an enormous stretch of water.

## Euclid Avenue

Anna Angeletti hires a piano
to satisfy the peculiar demands
of the visitors from England.

Stars are shining brightly
as a desperate Keats
tries to finish 'Death On The Piazza'
and comes up instead with Chapter 9
of *The Boys Book of Myths*.

Life, for some people, is not special. Advice:

'If you're going to identify with characters
in the books you read
be careful what you read.'

The crescent moon
catches a gleam of red sky
and someone is doing the monthly accounts
to avoid reading
some dull poetry. Tell me,

do you think
*My Tedious Life*
is a good title
for a book?

It's been used before
but a long time ago
and what Keats said
about filling some other body
reminds me I have a job to go to.

In some parts of the world
people believe that doing nothing
is the same as being everything;

in other parts of the world
people believe that life is all
steady progress toward death.

Let's face it,
if clarity is what you seek
you are not going to find this
kind of stuff very helpful.

Here on Euclid Avenue
a fantastic bird of many colours
has every question and every answer
but is having trouble matching them up.

The houses are brilliant
and have all we're ever going to need
but living in them
is a trial.

## The Beloved

If you've got something to say to me
then put it in a letter. Trust that I don't
adopt Coleridge's mode of dealing with an extensive
correspondence: open none, answer none.
Anyway, let me tell you,
our kid got snagged on the barbed wire and
since then things have been pretty hectic,
too pretty hectic for me
to take any notice of stuff coming in from without.
Have you ever seen
the damage barbed wire can do?
George said once he had a really great sheep
skin ripped to shreds out near Polstead. Anyway,
the doll's hospital, which is all we have here,
couldn't cope.
What's that you flash across
Constable Country at me from your point of vantage
using a bit of broken mirror to throw glints
of sun, resourceful as ever?
'Help. Am caught in elephant trap, I mean elegant trap
of eloquent domesticity. Have also lost
all those cassettes you recorded for me.'
Okay. I'll sing for you. Listen:
I think our postmen are terrific but misguided.
I want our kid to be a thug.

## The Inheritance

The theatres are impersonal and expensive,
rail terminals are dangerous places after dark.
Bankers hoard such immense wealth
men look up to them as gods. But,
as the gods deserved adulation not always, so too
these men of whatever it is, wherever it was,
how it is now.
When maps are delivered
receive them with grace.
The whisper of the ocean is behind each sacred moment;
when heroes depart for another country only the song
                    of solemn men remains.
Take care not to inherit inertia before your time.
Remember how much you forget each day:
the name of that man, what was it?
The cost of that meal, what? The books
on those shelves, did you read them?

## The Evidence

Item: he fell from the horse as gun music
filtered through the walls of the empty butterfly
enclosure. Eyewitnesses said the fall was
graceless, a sack of beans being tipped off
the back of a truck on to the warehouse floor.

We are left to ponder a few things
between the departure of the ambulance
for the infirmary and the arrival of the wine
from the songster vineyards of Bulgaria:

Item: who was that ugly bloke seen leaving the vicarage,
a chorister under each arm? Corky McCorcindale said that he
looked like the man on page 137 of Agatha Christie's
*The Murder of Roger Ackroyd*.

Item: the question mark hanging
over the authenticity of the alleged cloud
seen swallowing the sunlight of the dale.

Item: 49 out of 51, which is an overwhelming majority.

Item: the harmony of a little stream of incessant goodbyes.

Item: the indiscretion of being
caught outside Arturo's Dancette arm-in-arm.

Item: her dress
described by those who saw it
as 'greenfinch blue'.

Item: all the things I enjoy these days only stir up guilt.

Item: from left to right in the photograph: Malcolm Innes, sales
representative from The Eastern Press Company, Mr Alan Huffey of
The News Shop, and Mrs Pearl Gibson of Wilberforce Street, winner of
Sebastian the Giant Musical Teddy Bear.

Item: look, I don't want to
rummage in his room while he's away.

Item: the suspicious patrol car music,
and Officers Smith and Wesson 'off duty forever'.

Item: it'd be ungallant of me to take advantage of his accident
even though I think he's the collective arsehole of a
thousand flying pigs.

Item: I cannot be a juggler of lives.

Item: if all the world's a stage
then it's decent to be on it,
eating the dust of travel.

Item: eyewitness accounts of flight and escape.

Item: 'The Problem Symphony', and its lack of a tune.

Item: the legion dancers of the rodeo,
and the vultures
waiting on the branches of the trees.

Item: *The Science of Luck* (2 vols.) by Egil Skallagrimsson.

Item: the mad horse has become a folk hero more great
than The Window Cleaner in The Bank of Evening.

Item: the sadness of the departure lounge.

Item: absence was summoned, ladies and gentlemen,
and, as usual, has proved his guilt by not showing up.

# Stuff I Knew

I knew she had been seeing someone
else but I gave her the car keys
anyway. I knew God was dead but I
still sent him a Valentine's card.
I knew what happiness was but I
couldn't let that get me down.
I knew my future was behind me
but I set to the task body and
soul. I knew people misunderstood
but I'd always wanted to be popular
and much-loved. I knew the fat was a
flame but I had immense faith in the fire
brigade. I knew the roads were bad but
my aeroplane was in the hangar having
its wings fixed. I knew Ernest
Hemingway was a great novelist
but I still thought his books stank.
I knew my parents were not made of
stone but I was never able to get
blood out of them. I knew George
had his problems but I was sure mine
were worse. I knew I wasn't going to get
to heaven but I went for the interview
with an open mind and my life
laid out on a plate. I knew
I was on Dead-end Avenue with no
hope of reprieve but you had to
see the funny side. I knew they were
going to repossess everything but
none of it was mine so what the hell.
I knew my attitude was not good
but I also knew people who
admired my style. Also I knew
the habit was a killer but you
only live once. I knew the lorry
was headed for me but I took

no evasive action. I knew it was
a mistake because I knew a mistake
when I saw one, I'd seen so many.

## A Thin White Man

Night and its black sky
and white snow is falling. You can't
see the road, but the middle of the field
has just smacked you on the nose. A
sense of direction is a wonderful thing,
if you are the sort of man who can find
one. Wet rain lands on the hat on your
head and you can count the drops as they
fall: one, seven, four, nine. Watching
your watch (lucky it has a luminous
dial!) you observe time casually
pass you by. You can count the seconds,
and even the years: four, nineteen,
forty-two, four again. A man walks
his black dog in the black night
and they leave a trail of holes
in the white snow. The field is dark,
and you don't expect it to brighten up
just because dawn's coming. Thunder
and lightning are forecast and sadness
can be depended upon. One moment
in this life it snows, then it rains,
then it snows again. Life's like that,
and can be trusted to stay like that.
Darkness blanks out any light there
may have been. A thin white man
in snow may or may not be invisible,
but he is quiet. Listen: Nothing.

## The Surface Under Glass

Some things you should not touch:
an elephant apoplexied beyond recall,
for instance, or an aeroplane so many
leagues under the sea that it's
further than your imagination's range.
A furious mother is another,
and misplaced arrows are even more.
Faces turned inwards, idle hands held
behind the back, observation posts
manned by imbecile boys, a loser's
wager, ponderous offspring of men
carved out of dead trees, these also
are some of the things you should not
touch. You should not touch aristocrats
(though you may take any money they
have on them), nor should you touch
churchmen and members of private clubs;
green and red are colours you should
not touch, and the numbers forty-two
and 31. The sun when it is just risen,
the sun when it is just set, and all
other unbelievably hot things. Also, a
juggler in mid-juggle. A liar in mid-
lie. An ocean liner so far up in
the sky that clouds obscure the
Plimsoll Line. Another thing you
should not touch is a mountain when
it is moving, since this means that
times and all omens are bad. A gun
found in long grass you should not
touch, nor manacles upon a severed
limb. A fallow field, virgin soil,
these should not be touched. A verb
in the middle of its doing, an
adjective in the middle of its
description, and workmen at lunch,

these should not be touched. Father
burning his mouth in fury, anger
turning into iron, love melting into
uselessness, these also should not
be touched. And then the heart. Song
of the open door, the dream of
impossible wealth, dust on dreams,
and a dream house, these should not
be touched. Furthermore, the diamond
of night, the blood in the water,
the minute hand and the second chance,
and a crown on a fool's head. Further:
skin, flesh, hide, and the already
mentioned heart. These are some of
the things that should not be touched.

# Hot News From A Cold Place

Bernie Winters is dead and Lennie Summers is in mourning.
Nobody has written an obituary for Bernie Winters, tears
And laughter, and Lennie Summers is in mourning. There is
Not going to be a Bernie Winters retrospective on TV and
Lennie Summers is in mourning. They're not repeating even
One of the *Tonight with Bernie Winters* TV shows, and Lennie
Summers is in mourning. Bernie Winters had a brother,
The closeness of family, and Lennie Summers is in mourning.
*My Life with Bernie Winters* is out of print and Lennie
Summers is in mourning. Bernie Winters is dead,
And Johnny Thunders, and the world of variety substantially
Diminished, and Lennie Summers is in mourning.
*Man of Laughter, Man of Tears* will not now be made,
Bernie Winters is dead, and Lennie Summers is in mourning.
Corridors to possible worlds, the smiling variety, Bernie
Winters, and Lennie Summers is in mourning. No more
A million smiles, Bernie Winters, worry hardly at all,
And Lennie Summers is in mourning. *My 500 Best Gags* by Bernie
Winters, seasons are passing, time flieth like an arrow by day
Through sunlight and cloud and imagination and Lennie Summers
Is in mourning. Bernie Winters is dead, doors closing doors
Opening, and Lennie Summers is in mourning. Bernie Winters.

# The Real New Criticism

So we moved to the Isle of Wight
With a case of un-read books,
A box of matches and a pack of
Firelighters. We knew everything
There was to know about aggression
And were very aggressive. I had
A brand new Sekonda watch,
You wore a fragrance called 'Distance'.
I said 'Art' was about precisely that, and
Sea breaking upon an undiscovered shore.
I opened the case of books and
The odour of a disappearing world
Punched me 'Biff!' on the nose.
I felt sick, I had more important
Things to say and struck a match.
The books burned like bloody fuck.

'Those books burned like bloody fuck,'
You said, as we lay in the after-
Glow of brief sexual intercourse.
'Art is redundant these days, and TV
Is real communication.' I got out
Of bed and put on my new Doc Marten's
And you got out of bed and put on
An MC Hammer LP. 'We didn't need
The firelighters,' I said. 'But we might,'
You said. 'Yes, you're right.'
'I'm always right.' 'Not always.'
'Fucking am.' 'Fucking aren't.'
'Bollocks.' 'Fuck off.' 'Fuck you.'

# Bliss

For Rebecca & Dale

The Wedding-Guest has been duped.
Everybody's duped by the glittering eye:
What they said would never happen has happened,
What they said would happen has not happened.
You can't trust anybody these days:
These days what people say
Isn't worth the paper it's written on.
Even the paper isn't as good as it used to be.
You used to be able to trust paper.
In those days you could trust paper,
You could trust ink,
You could trust a man's dark and doleful moods,
You could trust the poet's tongue
And you could trust the sound of music.
The bassoon would play,
The Wedding-Guest would beat his breast,
And someone would remind someone else that
You only in those days had to talk to a girl six times
And they made you marry her. Great days.
Great days and great ways.
Something to believe in: The Great
Chain of Being and the Music of the Spheres.
Cherubim, Seraphim, no mention
Of credit cards, and women were angels though
Wedlock was the Devil. Great days those days,
But it's not good to cast longing looks
Backwards lingeringly though enjoyment should be
Grasped when seen, for it is but fleeting.
We drive faster but don't get there any quicker.
A man used to be able to trust his horse.
Now he doesn't have a horse, and the Wedding-Guest,
Standing still, says Progress is not moving forward.
Don't look at me like that.
Promises made under duress aren't real promises.
I know how big your brother is. In

My day brothers were even bigger
And didn't need machetes or machine guns.
Don't talk to me about courage.
Okay. You can talk to me about courage
If I can talk to you about cowardice.
All tragedies are finish'd by a death.
Byron said that.
All comedies are ended by a marriage.
Byron said that also.
The most happy marriage I can picture
Or imagine to myself would be
The union of a deaf man to a blind woman.
Coleridge said that.


I know you own the corner shop. I want to see
The accounts. You have to talk about money.
If we don't talk about money now
It'll be too late and it'll be
All there is to talk about. Silence
Embraces us so suddenly: The Wedding-Guest
Sits still on the stone.
Once upon a time you could trust a stone.
In those days you could trust stone,
You could trust the weight around your neck,
You could trust your neck on the block,
You could trust life to be a story
Barely worth the telling,
The story to have a beginning
A middle and an end, and the end to be happy
Or miserable and most probably in hospital.
Now you don't know. Nobody knows anything
Any more. There's so much to know
And it's too much and nobody knows
Nothing. Look at us. We wanted to be
Together. God knows nothing
Any more and he never knew why
We wanted to be together. We read
*Lolita*,

*The Tempest*, and
*Remembrance of Things Past*
In bed,
In deckchairs in bed,
In silence in bed,
In exotic clothing in bed,
In desperation in bed,
And in the end our eyes went. Our eyes went,
Our hair fell out, our limbs atrophied
And our tongues turned to leather.
But we had the kids. The kids were the Sun,
The Moon, the unending voice of the ocean
And its whisperings of eternity,
And a drain on our limited resources.
We had the photographs of the Big Day,
Of the numerous Bad Days,
And of days with far too many hours in them.
The Wedding-Guest turned from the bridegroom's door
And was hit by a truck. In those days
We were happy and innocent,
Now we are more sad, more wise.
The Wedding-Guest died, and we went to his funeral.
It made us think of our place in
The World, the State of the World,
The End of the World, and I
Couldn't be sure I'd turned off the gas.
I kind of hoped I hadn't.

# From a Recluse to a Roving I Will Go

First version of first story:
Title: A Recluse's Life Is Okay By Me.
Opening scene: stone-wrenching wind,
Moaning of forlorn and lost sheep,
Bewilderment in urban landscape,
Clouds cloaked across vengeful sky,
Firewood soaked by afternoon rains.
Pile of unopened mail on oak table,
Telephone ringing going unanswered,
Damn well didn't ask to be born,
The future ill-starred,
Past beyond remembrance,
Footsteps coming downstairs heavy.
Cup of coffee in kitchen,
Piles of laundry in each corner,
Applications for work abroad,
Photographs of unlikely women,
Clothes by *Man of Our Time*,
Books by unpronounceable East Europeans,
Estimates for car repairs heartbreaking.
Silence in dark moments at noon,
Friends laughing in other towns,
Milk turned in the refrigerator,
Nothing after life but death,
Nothing interesting to say about death,
Time flieth like an arrow,
Everything has a name except this,
Except this useless emotion.
Anger flaring into brilliance,
Frustration splintering like ice,
Life's little loops,
Life's stupid ironies,
Life's comic cuts,
Life's dead ends,
Life's open heart surgeries,
Life's great chip shop closed when you're hungry.

Favourite colour – green,
Favourite food – green,
Colour of jealousy and envy – green.
Visit from incompetent doctor,
Rain lashing against glass,
Power cut thanks to poor government.
Omens bad,
Tempers worse.
Blood oozing from bank statement,
White linen in neat folds on bed,
Wood shavings in carpet slippers,
Hay in the bed,
Silence in the bed,
Wallpaper on the outside walls,
An American prairie in the bed,
Silent moon at dawn,
Anagrams in breakfast cereal.
Dream,
Nightmare,
Fantasy,
Imagination,
Delusion,
Flight of fantastic Lagoon Bird.
Bawling of infant lungs,
Choir of angels,
Hint of Mr. Cleaver, Family Butcher,
The agony and the ecstasy,
The book of the film,
Translations into several languages,
Oceans breaking on a thousand shores,
Innocence and guilt and ignorance,
Week's wages on a useless horse,
Year's salary on a useless quest,
Sleep of the supine,
Kiss of the dead,
Love of the musically illiterate,
Love of the visually illiterate,
Love of the literally illiterate,

The last man out of here won't get out of here alive,
Uselessness of any word,
Speechless in the stained glass of night.

•

Second scene: morning:
Pigs lost in fog,
Postman found murdered in lane,
Bad news from army cousin in Ireland,
Cat hanging from tree,
Midwife mumbling unintelligibly,
Smoke curling from pile of smouldering smocks,
Hollering from crib,
Wife still refusing to enter the action.
Dawn's despair,
Breakfast blend in the coffee machine,
Detectives in the shrubbery.
Evidence of illegal entry,
Footsteps on rained on concrete,
Shadows on private life,
Hat missing from head in mirror,
Bulb missing from light in bathroom,
Sense missing from every waking moment,
Misunderstanding of Euclid's chief theories,
Incomprehension of looking on beauty bare,
Television covered in dust,
Power restored at nine,
Prayers rising into gloomy sky,
Religion lost and found and lost again,
Stranger in the house,
Realisation that life is now changed a lot.

•

Statement from the Divinity: 'Life's great.'

•

Swine found impersonating tramps on motorway,
Interrogation of swine,
Arrest of swine for murder of postman,
Passing of law forbidding persecution of swine,
Swine released pending public enquiry,
Child utters first words,
First words are either pig, pug, or rugby club.
Bedclothes steaming,
Recollection that something is forgotten,
Books burning in supermarket trolley in garden,
Someone reminds someone of someone else,
The wide world,
The far distance,
Pile of unopened mail covering hall floor,
Telephone disconnected as bill unpaid,
Grandparents arrive from Scotland,
Complaints Department opened in guest bedroom,
Blood and dirt under fingernails,
Holidays on South Coast recalled,
Iron filings under pillow,
Orange turning green in fruit bowl,
Cat turning green in tree,
Lagoon Bird takes flight for China,
Unreal women and urgent imagination,
*Selected Cantos of Ezra Pound*,
Two hours sleep in last thirty-six hours,
One moment of peace scheduled in next twenty years.
Pink sky of early evening,
Empire of declining influences,
Silence and beer,
Optimism and despair,
Eyes cloaked in layers of skin and loathing,
Misunderstanding of notion of responsibility,
Clarity like a bell cracking the silence,

Innocence in white,
Guilt in black,
Misinterpreted sense of humour,
Sense of self,
Sense of life,
Sense of what is nonsense.


•


Fourth scene, third missing, similar story:
Title: *Will I Ever Get To Go A Roving?*
Closing scene:
Forlorn and moaning lost souls,
Bewildered and urban,
Longing for escape,
Wrapped in cloak of solitude,
Afternoon pain lasting into middle of next week,
Weeks running into months and years,
Men running into mists of unreal women,
Men running into oblivion off high cliffs,
Men running into old friends in graveyards,
Men running into trouble,
Men running into brick walls,
Men running into the distance,
The distance nearing,
Men running blindly into it.
Men becoming consumed with misunderstandings.
Men becoming consumed by all-consuming passions.
Men becoming consumed by mistakes.
Men becoming consumed with evening meal.
Men honing art of self-pity to perfection,
Men taking imaginary burden to Olympian heights.
Floorboards curling in damp of autumn,
Paint peeling off prow of ship,
House falling down around ears,
Oil dripping from sump to tarmac,
Leaves dropping from boughs to green green grass,
Socks turning into soil in composted corners,

A different government,
The same balls up,
Refusal to listen to screams in night's deep,
Option of opting out refused and refused,
You didn't ask to be born,
Dogs barking in murmuring backyards,
Neighbours hanging baskets from caravans,
Old man sweeping lawn with ragged cardigan,
Rust flaking from combine harvester,
Ocean lapping at doorstep,
School closed,
Shops to let,
Pavements cracked,
Railway abandoned,
Man falls off ship into dock and never seen no more,
Bus late,
Factory derelict,
Bank collapsed,
Didn't have no money in it anyway,
Police corrupt,
Church corrupt,
Government corrupt,
Car fucked,
Evergreens no longer able to inspire sense of rhapsody,
Pissed off with career,
Someone calling name from kitchen,
Someone calling name from distant village,
Someone calling name from frozen bed,
Someone calling name from serious balcony,
Someone calling name from patio,
Someone calling name from shrubbery (The Fanny Price Walk),
Someone calling name from blackest night,
Someone calling name from abandoned restaurant,
Someone calling name from brilliant farm,
Someone calling name from *The Sunday Times Atlas of the World*.
Hang it all,
If you don't study, that's your fault.
Never had any ambition,

Had nothing to say,
Could say nothing,
Grew hysterical,
Grew hot,
Grew cold,
Grew indifferent,
Stopped growing.
Come home from work, house is gone.
Come home from work, family's gone.
Come home from work, want to go back to work.
Come home from work, God is dead.
Hang it all.
Hang it all and hang it all.

# His Story

If you insist I tell the truth, I went to sea to flee my
family. Living in that ramshackle house by the harbour
was getting me down. Okay, I didn't give much
thought, any thought at all, to whether or not it was
getting my wife and kids down too. She had her part-
time job cleaning at the inn, and the kids seemed to
delight everyone, everyone except me, that is. I'd see
the boats and the ships, and hear the sailors talk about
this, that and the other, and their words were like
flowers in a wilderness, the ocean a magnet to my iron
heart. Any road, I did it on the spur of the moment,
sort of, even though I'd been thinking about it for ages.
'The Angel' was bound for Bombay, I'd had a bit too
much to drink perhaps, and no, I didn't say Goodbye
and thinking about it now fair wrecks my head. But
what's done is done and it can't be undone. I don't
know if I can ever go back. Since I've been at sea I've
changed a lot and the people who knew me back then
probably wouldn't know me now even if they had a
mind to. I read a lot, and I've thought long and hard,
and I've learned that unto the pure all things are pure,
but I don't know where that leaves me. Gertrude Stein
said that a rogue is a rogue is a rogue, but I swear that
now my intentions are honourable and my ends of the
most admirable. There is a prayer –

'Lord,
May the Sky
Be constant azure overhead,
And the Ocean a murmuring
Never melancholy friend;
To all good wishes allow
A flowering of fulfilment.
May Comradeship, Loyalty,
Love and Compassion
Be our guides to the edges

*Of the discovered world.*
*May we bear Tempest,*
*Storm, Disease and Trial*
*With strength and dignity,*
*And should Evil threaten*
*Our bow give us spines*
*Of tempered steel.*
*We give ourselves*
*To you, Lord.'*

- and The Bible bids us pray without ceasing. I do what I can. I used to wish that the cabin boy would beg to share my bed and turn out to be a girl, but no more. I pray that my life be transformed into a neural calm, and that I be granted amiable and rewarding converse with wave and star, that a mild acceptance grace my every breath. I already accept the existence of miracles in this world.

# Guide

From the War Memorial take the lane
past the vicarage and the abandoned orphanage.
Continue along until the municipal car park
is at your elbow. If the wind is from the East
you will be able to smell the canning factory.
Pause a moment here, for there
is a fine view across the meadows
to the Castle's ornamental gardens. Turn left
and plough straight ahead stopping for no-one.
Follow the brook up to The Long Wall,
follow the line of the wall westward, and enter
the Castle grounds through The Beggar Gate.
Be sure to shut it after you. There are things
we must keep in, things that have to be protected.
Have your documentation to hand
in case you are stopped by a member of staff.

In Reception you may be given
a blow-by-blow account of domestic strife
in Castle Baden. Alternatively, pick up a leaflet
in the entrance hall, with our compliments.
We have become philosophers since
the blush of virginity left our beds and our lives
became shrubs with more dead wood than living foliage,
and trust our tale will not blight your stay.

When Coleridge stayed here in 1802
he wrote to the effect that his heart was softened
and made worthy to indulge love and
the thoughts that yearn for humankind.
Be that as it may, there are innumerable walks,
and we advise shoes or boots with grip-soles
as the going can often be muddy and slippery.
The village nestles like an irritation
in a fold of land at the north-eastern edge
of The Nameless Hills.

Symbolists come here on field trips;
was the English countryside ever so brilliant?
The history of the village has been written down:
pick up a leaflet in the entrance hall.
There is fine watercolouring to be had
subject to written permission of the owners.

On Thursday evenings Mrs Poole comes in
to play piano, and attendance is obligatory.
We have learned that what we love cannot last,
that if bliss exists at all it is only at the bottom
of a pit of darkness. Mr Poole, dead these fifteen years,
was a great man who refused to trust
the air even when it was in his lungs.

Make the most of your stay here:
flights of incredible fancy increasingly have no place
in this life. Once there was magic.
The first Duke of Baden was able to conjure
a hunting party from the pages of the telephone directory,
his love letters smelled of slowly roasting oxen,
and on top of his wardrobe was a suitcase that had been
all over the Empire. Those days may be gone for ever
but we still have our imaginations.

Now, where are your keys?
Be sure to consider security at all times.
We offer an easy-to-read guide to this
and many other subjects of philosophical enquiry
in a special multilingual format. Pick up a leaflet
in the entrance hall, with our compliments.
Remember, our staff are always on hand to assist.

Finally, please be quiet: we have loved more than our lives
and now try to sleep as much as possible. Notice how
the mind is suddenly clouded but just as suddenly unclouded.

# A Hundred of Happiness

Okay: The Finger visits Paris and is entranced by its abandon.
On a river cruiser he falls in love with the notion of The Ripple.
Little does The Finger know that The Ripple has only a short
Time to live, and The Ripple is not used to having a close friend
In whom it can confide its loneliest secrets, its deepest regrets.
The Finger and The Ripple are together in the Parisian summer
And while it lasts there's no point in trying to deny their joy.

## Yes

She says that the world is a strange place
and the shops open weird hours, the hours
she is either asleep or on another planet,
and she says she used to believe that all
that could be expected of life was a climb
up a mountain and a scary roll down the
other side, and then she said that her mum
hadn't been the best mum in the world
but as mums go she supposed she wasn't so bad
but there had been moments when things
had got so awful her lack of interest in being alive
had been replaced by a strong desire to be dead,
and then she said she knew loads of people,
all of them men, who really all they wanted
to do was horrible stuff, and if you could
trust anybody in the world they were probably
going to be made of some kind of cloth,
stuffed with foam or cotton wool, and imported
from Taiwan, and then she said that all of
a sudden her life had been turned upside down
and all she could think of was happiness and
all she could think of was brilliant and she
was pretty knocked out by this strange feeling
and should she trust it. Well, should she?

# Against Madness

Put a frog in an anthill. Powder the skeleton,
Mix it with bat blood and dried flies, and make it
Into tiny buns. Bake a turtledove, then powder it
And add it to the wine of the woman you desire.
Take a donkey's ear and some oil and boil them
Together. Step upon they anger with thy heel and
Thy forefoot. Dissolve the brains and heart of a bear
In new wine. Take the gall of a male cat and
The fat of a hen all white, anoint the eyes
And see what others cannot see. Burn the hair
Of a black dog to powder and mix with mother's milk
And child's faeces. May what you see increase
And what you suffer cease. Bake 12 large earthworms
On a shovel and ground to powder. Drink
In a potion. Put black snails in a pot, add salt,
And bury it for nine days. Drink the juice of
Leaves of adder's tongue with distilled
Water of horse tail. Every morning eat a black spider
Between two slices of buttered bread. Anoint your eyes
With gall of cock. Congeal chicken blood
In a small goat's horn. Beat your own shadow with
A cane. Hanker thou after my body, my feet,
Hanker after my eyes, my thighs. Put a blade
Of grass in your mouth and turn to the east.
Fascinate a woman by giving her a piece of cheese.
Put nine drops of your fresh blood on a cloth
In which you will steam the food of the one
You love. ('Every moving thing I have held fast.
Eye and breath I have held fast. I have held fast
All limbs in the deep gloom of night.')
Burn part of a dress after you have
Perspired heavily into it and introduce the ashes
Into the food or drink of the man you desire.
Find a pair of dogs copulating, put a cloth over
Them, and give it to the girl you want. Thread
A needle with her hair and run it through the

Fleshiest limb of a dead man. Piss through
A wedding ring. Spit in your own bosom.
Take milk of a slut and saturate therewith
The spot wherever the hair is desired to grow.
Under a stone that is heavy do we cast thy anger.
Baptise a large toad. Stick pins into a sheep's heart.
Throw hair into the sea to start a storm. Tell your
Bad dreams to the sun. Wear a thumb cover made
From the ear of a black cat boiled in the milk
Of a black cow. At midnight take off your left shoe
And put manure on the big toe. Sit
A naked woman on a heavy stool in the yard.
This is for catching a large fish.

# The Other Position

How it is under the mother's wing: I'm going to learn
to ride a horse before I go to bed and dream of riding
on the back of a whale.

How it is under a cloud: I'm going to drink from a cup
made from the clay off your boots and let hot oil
course through my veins until I glow like a lamp on a
windowsill.

How it is under an avalanche: I'm going to rub my
thighs with salt from the kitchen cupboard and con-
gratulate myself on the warmth of my stove.

How it is under the waterfall: I'm going to fall in love,
argue with myself, and then propose to the girl in the
liquid necklaces.

How it is under the full moon: I'm going to run my
tongue over your skin and let other men frown in their
sleep.

How it is under the cosh: I'm going to bathe my hands
in ink and watch the words drip off my fingertips on to
the page.

How it is under siege: I'm going to invent machines of
sadness and joy and sell them at a massive profit; buy
them at your peril.

How it is under observation: I'm going to daub my
cock in candle grease and then go look for the matches.

How it is under no illusion: I'm going to set fire to my
employer's office and watch the fire brigade at work.

How it is under a lot of self control: I'm going to have six cups of strong coffee, give some stuff a deal of thought, and then retire gracefully.

How it is under a misapprehension: I'm going to have a hot bath, put on my fleecy pyjamas, and go to bed with a good book.

## Lies I Must Remember

It wasn't me who forgot to cancel the papers
so the news kept coming and coming and coming.

It wasn't me who ordered
the deep fat fryer from the Kay's catalogue,
setting off the sequence of events
that led to the burning down of our house.

It wasn't me who said
'Love is for ever, and forever is way past my bedtime.'

It wasn't me helping the police with their enquiries
into where The Tree of Curiosity had been planted,
and who planted it.
And why.

It wasn't me who noticed that Lust,
passing Beauty on the stair,
tumbleth head over heels like an arse.

It wasn't me who put an elegant chair
leg through the TV screen.

It wasn't me arrested for outrageous handsomeness.

It wasn't me who underwent major surgery
for what doctors described as
'uneven opinions, and too much speaking out loud of
his own mind.'

It wasn't me chalked
CLOUDS OF HAPP
on the sky to show
the marvellous almost in rea

## Adventures With Everything

Awakening into daylight the housekeeper daydreams
and becomes a shepherd shepherding
a flock of carpet sweepers sweeping across
the lush green grass of a pasture. The
poet becomes the stone about which he eulogises,
and the scissors become the event
they are shaping. A paper
bird becomes a black sheet of rain,
astonishing prospects become a dirty mirror
and a worried face becomes an exercise book
filled with algebraic equations.
An explorer in the desert becomes the pyramids
he is looking for, the scientist becomes the last
experiment and everything is revealed.
Night turns into morning, morning into afternoon,
afternoon into evening and evening into night;
daylight into dusk, twilight into darkness into dawn,
and awakening into daylight King Tidy becomes a world
authority on Chaos Theory, the best
laid plans become a pile of bricks
left out in the rain, and the borders
of the kingdom become words on paper.
The mad pianist becomes an astronomer
looking at the moon, the moon becomes a man
whose fortune is made in Heaven,
and a man looking for somewhere
to hide becomes the dark corner.
The card player becomes the Tarot,
and the fool plucks an orange from a tree
as the crowd waits for a lucky card to be handed them
on a plate. Great civilisations pop up
and pop down again as quickly as each page
of The Book of The World is turned,
and coloured balloons on the end of
lengths of twine become newly-discovered planets
upon which life as we know it may or may not exist.

## Where Bears Walk

I've been thinking if this is the town
we're going to live in I should tell
my friends what it's like. So friends,
know there are buskers in the market place,
that there is some trading, the sun shines
on the traders as little as it shines on
traders anywhere else in the kingdom,
some intellectual property is exchanged
but not very much, and a deal of idle chatter
falls, leaves drifting down to the pavement
to be trodden underfoot by the inevitable
sports shoe and Doc Marten. Men
and women from distant lands are rare,
the clinking of coin and rustle of paper money
more common, and travellers with tales
to tell pass through but don't stay very long.
Know that the girls' coloured hair is
caught by the sun when it shines
and shines in it, that when business
has been done much remains still to be done
tomorrow, the day after and the day
after that, and that in this as in so many
things this town is the same as
any other. People sit around
wondering what the future might hold
for them, but when a crystal ball
is called for none is forthcoming; the future
will come, someone has written on a wall,
and there's nowt one can do to alter it,
but if a world you imagine is what you know
and love and rest comfortable in the bosom of
then that's fine. This is a state of mind
through which bears walk, but you should know
they are harmless, dogs stand guard
at the wall, and there was a wire fence
separating honesty and deceit but it's been

taken down long since; there was
a well-oiled machinery of men and women
in case of catastrophe
but now all that's needed is friends
you can collapse in the back of.
Only here does music fill the air, only
here do different tongues speak
in many languages and different eyes see
the invisible. Only here is there no lack
of fine sights in the way of birds and beasts,
citizens dressed in white clothes
of good omen, nine times nine white horses
and stars that shine throughout the day.
Know that only here a crowd
gathers to welcome the sun and cheers
like crazy when it catches the girl's
coloured hair, and when the hair flares
the bears walk by her side and they're smiling.

# Sense of a Horse

The horse broke into the china shop because he mistook
it for a stable. Police enquiries often lead to false arrest.
Perfection is difficult to attain even when aimed for.
A smile graces a girl's face in the evening, but by the time
next morning comes it has been replaced by an expression of
disappointment. If the sun shines on calm lake water it is safe
to take the rowboat out, though be careful not to overload
the food hamper. Perhaps it is best if one of us stays at
home in case the telephone rings. We each have five senses:
sense of guilt, sense of loss, sense of the absurd, sense
of bewilderment and sense of direction. What was going through
the mind of the horse as it was led away by the young constable
cannot be guessed at. Nobody can understand anybody else,
and sometimes it's not worth even having a crack at working
it out. We are able to function in all sorts of different
social situations but are not comfortable in any of them.

# ARISING

## Parried Endlessly

If poems can't slug it out
with kids and mayhem and shopping life
overdrafts and broken cars and jobs
they're not worth shit: of course
sometimes it's necessary to be sleepy
and on that day a sleepy poem is the true poem
Sometimes one is filled with questionings:
> The Grand Canal
> Endless Life
> Difficulties and Exultations
> The Wasted Land
> Friend
> The Piano
> Rationality
> Paradise Regained

but these are only the answers
and they're not of much use
It's the space between the blocks of words
we love and inhabit
The anticipation of what's coming next
neither empty nor silent
Your expectations seem to be eternally denied
You think that's bad
but it's not bad
though we're given to understand it's necessary

## Overwhelm

This is what we do and it's so filled with character as if
yet again the sea and yet again the sky and also again the
'all we believe in has evaporated and been replaced by
a lorry load of strangers and their strangenesses.'

Please don't ask for an explanation: it can't be but if it could
what was explaining would have already slipped away and
become worthless and irrelevant. The last thing said
may not be the last thing thought: thought may not be
what you think, which is not an original thought

but if you think about it it's overwhelming:
this is what we don't do, and it's blank a lot of the time and
how do you explain over the border the land of strangers
where what you don't know falls off trees.

There was more than we could take in then we remembered:
we've forgotten

## Who May Offer

Always until the end of life looking for
record shops and bargains of noise because
this silence is just too quiet. Do anything
you want to do. When you were just looking
you were just looking gorgeous.
It's not, the ugly can't comprehend,
easy to be this handsome.
These spectacles seem to be faulty.

## Abandoned

The countryside was invented. Tradition
was broken with. The moon was passed on
the left-hand side. It's easy being this clever.
Caring is not an aberration. Feeling is
with more than your body. Often what we
are told is great is not great. Or our sadness
is. Do anything so long as it drives
someone bonkers. They may be laughing
at you. Swans and geese are different.
Always be in part an actor. This code does
not unlock this lock. A foreign language is
only okay if you understand it. Mathematics
holds us together. Happiness is
fickle. Poems don't have to rhyme.

## It's No Good Being Imaginary

It's no good being imaginary. Someone might stop
thinking about what you look like, or
they might just stop thinking about the palace
in which you are living so long
as they are thinking. This might be a good place
to stop: a weekend or an overnight turning
into a long and miserable life always together.
Boy, that's a really big bed you could get lost
in it and not speak to one another, married happily.

# A Time A-Roving

After all this comes this. It's happening
again, and still we've not gotten used to
it. Fucking life. Optimism and despair.
The bed is unstable, as if on a small ship
on a mighty sea. But the dreamings are too big
and can't be accommodated, not right now,
not in this mood, this end of year mood

Here comes the next phase, happy and
jaunty. We tried hoisting the bed on
to our shoulders and it fell apart. Guitars
strum optimistically, repetition being okay.
Stars shining.

And in the background some people are
eyeing us anxiously, waiting for the failure.
There by the side of the everlasting sea.

## Surprise

Boo! This is now what you expect
or this is not what you expect
and anyway you are not here the joke
misfired Was any of this at all
planned? The questions are baffling:
old as the years accumulate
what adds up at last leaves us
gawping like idiots at the circus
One day stood on the aquaduct
thinking about the new you
Suddenly it was the 20th century again
it seems so long ago but it was only
yesterday You got new hair a new look

## Rough Manner

As hopeless as literary folk gathered together
in a dockyard, listening to hopeless poems
(of which in the world there are countless)
Here's one, about a chair:
No, this is a cringe too far
Oh, alright then, here's the last three lines:
'I light a cigarette,
inhale deeply, sigh and press
my bottom to his nicely padded seat.'
The poem stars Kenneth Williams and Barbara Windsor.
Actually it doesn't but if it did it would be better.

## In a Season

Home is not where it once was
but it's better and it's funny

Here at year end a few chapters
into the new book that will not be
without its suspenseful moments

Hold your breath
but not for too long

## Get Angry

When the hairdrier broke
there was someone on hand
to lend her theirs. They had
no use for it anyway,
being bald. On inspection,
it was only the fuse had gone
and now they have two
hairdriers, which is quite
extravagant. There are
some people in the world
who have none at all.

## Mimic You

Oh cry, why don't you cry. There's nothing wrong
with crying yourself to sleep.
The only way sometimes (after a glass of milk
and a dry biscuit and the pills that are supposed to
make you someone else) put your feet up
Try really hard to relax Put some effort into it

## Enjoying a Lift

This beautiful road. Where does it go?
What name do the folk who travel it
assume? The horizon with buildings on it
and windows alight in the night
faces at them if you could see
Birds nest under the eaves
Who invented the white line separating
the comings and goings? Who
invented dusters? Is there really
anyone who understands any of this?
Imagine her, all woman, by the side
of the beautiful road

## Some Breakfast

Sun at this time of day is a blessing often
ignored and your opening eyes
unseeing and still dreaming
Don't go to work today
Don't ever go again

## Light on a Biblical City

Sun at this time of day
opens the poetry shop
but there are no customers
which isn't surprising
Have you seen what's in the window?
Mmm – this starberry lip balm
is delicious it takes your mind off
bad things though they return
Sun at this time of day
all it does is remind us of the windows
they need cleaning
It's all work if you want to see through

## Like a Completed Crossword

There is a complex system of thought
and afterthought but what in the end
it boils down to is the usual human fuck up:
Here's a clue:
the day came and she knew
she had to tell him the game was up.
And tomorrow the secret is out

## Artist in the Modern Style

All one can do is buckle down and work
and not care if one is taken notice of –
crackling with wit and handsome as a bug

He stumbled from rock to stone
then another rock. Some are so huge
one may divert around another island
to a country where difference is usual

Where they make everything up
and it almost makes a complete picture
the trees along the riverbank
adjoining the historic castle

And when it's up in the air it's up
and when it's down on the ground it's down
(and when it's only half way up
it's neither up nor down)

All one can do is buckle down and work

# Arising

And whilst it was given unto us to live in solitary confinement
while the wolf was at the door
and we were willing and able to greet the sun with minds resigned
Here we go combing our hair in the bleakly windy winterland
We are used to kissing the ground as it rises to meet us
and waving farewell to those who are drowning
We write down our days in the sand by the sea
become philosophers
and walk on our hands in the world turned upside down
Our eyes are in the habit of closed in the blessèd weald
and as for the air it is only the fucking air
with our smallest breath in the centre of it all etc.
Every day one of our tasks is to concentrate
on the instant of ignition
though we have no idea what that means
Do you remember the time we sucked the moon from the sky?
No.
But we bowed and received
and it is given unto us to be younger than we are
Only this world can give us this and this act of faith
      And we believe in the inevitable
      when it is happening
      Submit to the irresistible
      when we are suffocating in its embrace
      Have faith in the unbelievable
      while we sit here waiting for it

# CONVERSATIONS WITH MYSELF
## selected reviews and notes 1984-1998

If these collected reviews and other writings have themes they probably have to do with the author's evolving discovery over the years of what poetry is, for him, and his struggle to articulate his thoughts about the poetry he likes and the poetry he doesn't. For Martin Stannard, reviewing has always been a process where he finds out what he thinks and questions himself. During this process what started out as gut reaction becomes sentences with words in them, ready to face readers and their questions.

Readers who care about contemporary poetry, and the current reception and perception of it, are sure to enjoy this book.

'...one of the liveliest books of criticism I've read. Criticism seems too academic a word: this is opinionated, funny and at times scurrilous prose that can find the kiss-me-I'm -poetical junk in a poet in less time than it takes him to write his own name. His disgust at pretentiousness and the dull is only matched by his enthusiasm for the truly good. ...more wit, style and pazzaz than a dozen Faber poets, or a brace of clever postmodernists hooked on Baudrillard.'
  *The North*

'I admire the way Stannard clearly states his position and, in so doing, allows the reader to follow his reasoning. He is sharp and illuminating.'
  *Tears in the Fence*

'Beneath the chatty and confident style lies an acute critical sense, a sharply observant mind, and a refreshing anger about the poetry scene.'
  *County Lit*

*Conversations With Myself* is available for £7.95, post free, from the publisher:
STRIDE PUBLICATIONS
11 SYLVAN ROAD, EXETER, DEVON EX4 6EW
*(cheques payable to 'Stride' please)*